A woman's beautiful character is determined by her spiritual life. The key to becoming a godly woman is fear of the Lord. Reverence for God is expressed in the submission to His will and is the beginning of knowledge. A woman who fears the Lord will be praised (Proverbs 31:30). She lives her faith. She is a beautiful woman of God. She has become a woman of virtue.

An eight-week, in-depth interactive Bible study for the woman who likes to linger in the Word.

Also by Rita Kroon:

*Letters from the Past*
*You Have Cancer – A Journey Through the Valley of the Shadow of Death*
*Praying the Scriptures*

# WOMANHOOD: BECOMING A WOMAN OF VIRTUE

An Eight-Week, In-Depth Bible Study

Rita Kroon

The Essence of a Woman Fashions
the Person She Will Become

CROSSBOOKS
PUBLISHING

*CrossBooks™*
*A Division of LifeWay*
*1663 Liberty Drive*
*Bloomington, IN 47403*
*www.crossbooks.com*
*Phone: 1-866-879-0502*



*First published by CrossBooks 11/05/2012*

*ISBN: 978-1-4627-2256-3 (sc)*
*ISBN: 978-1-4627-2255-6 (e)*

*Library of Congress Control Number: 2012920325*



*Printed in the United States of America*

*This book is printed on acid-free paper.*

For my daughters,
LaDawn, René, and Shelly
For Carol Patterson,
Mary Delk,
and
all ladies in Bible study

***What a joy to share***
***the Scriptures with***
***each of you!***

# Table of Contents

# Womanhood
# Becoming a Woman of Virtue

A woman who fears the Lord shall be praised.
Proverbs 31:30 (NIV)

## About the Study

The in-depth Bible study is geared toward the woman who likes to linger in the Word, and it is suitable for either an individual study or for a group setting.

Whether you choose the individual or the group option, I am delighted that you and I have this opportunity to discover the treasures that God has in store for us through the study of women of Old Testament times. On the eight-week journey, we will meet the first woman of Eden, dine with the queen of Persia, and meet several women in between.

As we embark on this expedition through the annals of history, we will discover that it is here that the basic lesson of cause and effect, choices and consequences, and obedience and blessing begins its consistent journey down through the centuries.

The women we will meet are, for the most part, ordinary beings. They would not make headlines in any history book but God's, because there are no unimportant people in God's sight. The fact that God recorded their stories for our learning reveals what He considers important.

Some of the choices and decisions these women face will replay themselves again and again in the history of humanity. As we get to know these women, their choices will challenge us, their faith will inspire us, their hardships will encourage us, and the lessons they learned will reflect a ready application for our own lives.

As we complete each day's assignments, we will come to know what the Lord is saying to each of us personally as we use the observation-interpretation-application method of study.

*Observation* asks questions about the basic facts—*who, what, when, where,* and *how. Interpretation* asks questions that delve into the meaning of the passage of Scripture. *Application* asks questions that will help us to discover the implication for our own personal growth in Christ Jesus.

We will seek the wisdom of the Holy Spirit as we compare Scripture with Scripture, make use of footnotes, look at different commentaries, and then apply to our lives what we have read and understood to be the revealed Word of God.

Each week's study lesson is devoted to one woman of the Old Testament and explores the background, culture, circumstance, and struggles of these women with lessons that are relevant to today's woman.

## Individual In-Depth Study

Five daily homework assignments require individuals to spend approximately thirty-five to forty minutes per day to complete. Personal application questions are at the end of each daily lesson.

## Group In-Depth Study

Participants will meet together once a week for a two-hour session with, ideally, six to seven women per small group to study and discuss the completed daily homework assignments. Questions are meant to help us *connect* with women of the Old Testament, *relate* to one another in class, and *hear* what the Lord is saying to each of us through His written word. Group discussion questions are at the end of each daily lesson.

# Introduction

The idea for this particular Bible study, *Womanhood: Becoming a Woman of Virtue,* was first relayed to me by my very dear friend and Bible study leader, Carol Patterson. She read the first two chapters of my book, *Letters from the Past,* and called me, saying, "Girlfriend, you have got to make this into a Bible study!"

The idea began to take a more definite shape when Mary Delk, Director of Women's Ministries at Bethlehem Baptist Church in Minneapolis, Minnesota, suggested that I write a women's Bible study. This was affirmed by the women in the study I was leading at the time.

As I researched and compared Scripture with Scripture, the first chapters began to emerge, and I realized that if I was to be a successful Christian author, my work must first and foremost bring honor to the Lord Jesus Christ. Secondly, it must draw others into a deeper walk of faith with Him through the study of His Word. I am reminded of the words of my pastor, John Piper, who said, "God is most glorified when we are most satisfied in Him." To honor the Lord and to be satisfied in Him was my motivation to write this Bible study, and I hope you also will "Do your best to present yourself to God as one approved, a workman who does not need to be ashamed and who correctly handles the word of truth" (2 Timothy 2:15).

I am delighted you have chosen to put on your sandals, pack your satchels, and journey with me through time and distance to meet and get to know eight women of the Old Testament so that we may apply to our lives the invaluable lessons we glean from each of them.

With God's Word as our map and the Holy Spirit as our guide, let's begin our quest of finding the treasures God has placed before us as we travel from the past to the present and from faceless portraits to a reflection of ourselves.

Welcome to the beginning of time!

*Rita Kroon*

# Week One
# In the Beginning

## Day One
## God Creates the Earth

## Day Two
## The Tempter Arrives

## Day Three
## Trouble in the Garden

## Day Four
## Dire Consequences

## Day Five
## Promised Savior

Day One

# God Creates the Earth

In the beginning, God created the heavens and the earth.
—Genesis 1:1

This verse is familiar to most people, but let's unpack this opening statement of God's Word and see if we can find our first hidden treasure.

What does the phrase "in the beginning" mean to you? ______________________________

______________________________________________________________

The word *beginning* in Genesis 1:1 is the natural meaning of the word with reference to time[1]—when time was introduced from the preexisting timelessness of antiquity. So "in the beginning" could be phrased to be the start of creation and marks the first interruption of the past endless eternity. In other words, time is introduced at the beginning of creation.

The writer of the gospel of John also started his letter with the words "in the beginning." However, John used this phrase to mean *eternity.* He wrote in John 1:1–3, "In the beginning was the Word, and the Word was with God, and the Word was God." "In the beginning" here refers to "before time began or timeless existence; continually existing prior to creation; prior to time." Verse 2 says, "He was in the beginning with God." The word *was* actually means "already in existence or eternal." Verse 3 records the words, "All things came into being by Him and apart from Him nothing came into being that has come into being."

The one who was in existence from eternity—prior to the creation of the world—is He who John describes as the One he and the other disciples have seen, heard, and touched. The Word of life was with the Father in eternity and was manifested to man, not at the creation of the earth, but two thousand years ago, when Jesus was born in Bethlehem.

According to John 1:14, 17, who is this Word who became flesh and dwelt among us, who was full of grace and truth? ______________________________

God became man—Jesus Christ, Son of God and Son of Man, fully God and fully man in one being!

What is He called in Revelation 19:13? ______________________________

Read 1 John 1:5. What message did the apostles hear from the Word of God?

______________________________ and

______________________________

Let's explore more deeply the meaning of eternity, which may help us to better understand the difference between eternity and when time began.

*Eternity*—"a timeless existence, a being or entity without change" is what is meant by eternity and not mere everlastingness or permanence through time. God, in His eternal being, is raised above time in His eternal absoluteness—and knows no changeableness. God is eternal, while as yet the world and time were not.[2] Eternity pertains to God; the words "in the beginning" of Genesis 1:1 correlate to when the earth was created.

Hebrews 1:10–12 (NIV) says,

In the beginning, O Lord, You laid the foundations of the earth,
and the heavens are the work of Your hands. They will perish,
but You remain; they will all wear out like a garment. You will
roll them up like a robe; like a garment they will be changed.
But You remain the same, and Your years will never end.

Paraphrase these verses in your own words.

______________________________

______________________________

In the beginning, God created the heavens and the earth (Genesis 1:1). Let's take a look at the word *God* as it appears in this verse.

God, or *Elohim,* can be used as a generic term for deity as well as a proper name most often used for the true God, as it is here. It can also be used for pagan gods and idols, however, as in Genesis 31:30 and Exodus 12:12.

> Laban speaking to Jacob: "And now you have indeed gone away because you longed greatly for your father's house; but why did you steal my gods?" (Genesis 31:30 NASB)
>
> The Lord speaking to Moses and Aaron: "For I will go through the land of Egypt on that night, and will strike down all the first-born in the land of Egypt, both man and beast; and against all the gods of Egypt I will execute judgments—I am the Lord." (Exodus 12:12, NASB)

The plural form of Elohim, as used in Genesis 1:1, indicates plentitude of power and majesty and refers to the true God and Creator of the heavens and the earth. But God is more than Elohim. According to Genesis 2:4, by what name is He called for the first time in the Scriptures? ________________

*Note:* Lord (YHWH—pronounced Yahweh) is the most significant name for God in the Old Testament. It has a twofold meaning: the active, self-existent one (Exodus 3:14) and Israel's Redeemer (Exodus 6:6). The name Yahweh occurs 6,823 times in the Old Testament and is especially associated with God's holiness (Leviticus 11:44–45), His hatred of sin (Genesis 6:3–7), and His gracious provision of redemption (Isaiah 53:1, 5–6, 10).

According to Exodus 3:14, who does God say He is? ________________________________

Read Hebrews 13:8. Who is the same yesterday and today, yes and forever? ________________

John 8:23–24, 28 and 13:19 all imply that Jesus is the I AM of the Old Testament (OT), but John 8:58 is explicit! Who does Jesus claim to be? ________________________________________

*Note:* "I AM" denotes absolute eternal existence, not simply existence prior to Abraham. It is a claim to be Yahweh of the OT. That the Jews understood the significance of this claim is clear from their reaction (John 8:59) to the supposed blasphemy. How did they react? ____________________

________________________________________________________________________________

In the beginning, God created the heavens and the earth. The Hebrew word *bara* means "to do or to make" (used in Genesis 1:25 and also of the entire creative activity in Exodus 20:11). Genesis 2:7 uses the word *yatsar,* which means "formed." The Lord God *formed* man of the dust from the ground.

It was said by those of the Middle Ages that there were seven wonders of the ancient world: the Pyramids of Egypt, the Hanging Gardens of Babylon, the statue of Zeus at Olympia, the Temple of Artemis at Ephesus, the Mausoleum at Halicarnassus, the Colossus of Rhodes, and the Lighthouse of Alexandria. Since then, the Great Wall of China, the Taj Mahal, and Stonehenge are among the icons tagged as wonders of the world.

Are you curious, as I am, if the ancient people considered the earth itself to be a matchless wonder? Those Middle-Agers recognized the wonders of the world brought recognition to man's achievements, but do you think they realized the earth itself ascribes glory to God, its Creator?

Let's peek behind the curtain of obscurity and watch the entire creation unfold before our eyes.

**Day 1** Genesis 1:3: God said, "Let there be ________." God separated the light from the darkness. *Note:* God did not separate the sun, which was created on the fourth day, but some fixed light source outside the earth. In reference to that light, the rotating earth passed through a day-night cycle, and it was so. He called the light ______________________________ and the darkness ______________________________.

**Day 2** Genesis 1:7: And God made the expanse and separated the waters which were below the expanse from the waters which were above the expanse. And God called the expanse ______________________________.

**Day 3** Genesis 1:9: God said, "Let the waters below the heavens be gathered into one place, and let the dry land appear." And it was so. And God called the dry land ______________________________ and the gathering of the waters He called ______________________________
Genesis 1:11: Then God said, "Let the earth sprout vegetation, plants yielding seed and fruit trees bearing fruit after their kind." And it was so.

**Day 4** Genesis 1:14: Then God said, "Let there be lights in the expanse of the heavens to separate the day from the night, and let them be for signs and for ______________________________, and for ____________ and ______________." And it was so. God made the greater light to govern the day and the lesser light to govern the night. He made the ______________________________ also. God placed them in the expanse of the heavens to give light to the earth.

Are you, like me, beginning to be awed once again with the tender care God used in creating the earth? Are you not equally amazed at the power of God to speak the heavens and the earth into existence? Do we not tremble at His might?

**Day 5** Genesis 1:20: Then God said, "Let the waters teem with swarms of living creatures, and let birds fly above the earth in the open expanse of the heavens." And it was so. Since there were no birds of prey or animals of prey, there was no bloodshed. Every living creature ate only green plants (see Genesis 1:29–30). God saw that all of creation was good and in perfect balance.

Go back and read Genesis 1:1–25. Using your imagination, describe what you think the newly created world may have looked like. ______________________________
______________________________
______________________________
______________________________

Can you picture lush vegetation and trees with new leaves like the ones of spring? Can you hear the myriad birds singing sweetly to their Maker? Do you see trees with several varieties of luscious fruit hanging in heavy clusters? Can you smell the fragrance of flowers gracing the landscape? Do you feel the fine mist that rose up to water the earth? Are you tempted to dip your toes into the cool, crystal-clear water of the rivers that flowed on the borders of Eden? Do you not just revel in the fact that there were no weeds? Everything existed in perfect harmony. There was no ecological upset, no global warming, no pollution, no ultra-violet rays doing damage. Nothing—just perfect and harmonious beauty!

For a complete account of creation, read Genesis 1–2, and for additional reading on creation for your personal enrichment, also read Isaiah 42:5, 45:18 and Psalm 102:25.

**Day 6** Genesis 1:26: Then God said, "Let us make man in Our image, according to Our likeness and let them rule over all the earth. God saved His masterpiece until last.

Read Genesis 1:26, 2:7. God created ______________________ in His own image. *Note: Us* and *our* are plurals of majesty. *Image* means likeness. Man was created in a natural and moral likeness to God. (When he sinned, he lost the moral likeness, which was his sinlessness, but the natural likeness of intellect, emotion, and will he still retained.) James 3:9 says, speaking of the tongue, "With it we bless our Lord and Father, and with it we curse men, who have been made in the likeness of God."

List three reasons why man was unique or distinct from animals. (Genesis 1:26–27, 2:7)

______________________________________________

______________________________________________

______________________________________________

______________________________________________

The word *yatsar* means "formed" and gives the picture of a potter at work, forming and molding with his hands the material he holds. (The same verb is used to picture the shaping of a people of a nation.) God formed man of the dust of the ground. God breathed (*napah*) into his nostrils the breath of life; man became (*hayah*) a living soul.

Read 1 Corinthians 15:47–49. Who is the first man from the earth? ____________________
Who is the first man from heaven? See John 6:38 and Philippians 3:20. ____________________

What special care did God use in the creating of man? Read Genesis 2:7. ____________________

______________________________________________

How did man become a living being? (Genesis 2:7) ______________________________

______________________________________________

What additional care did God as Creator use when he fashioned woman? (Genesis 2:21–22)

______________________________________________

______________________________________________

______________________________________________

Why is she called woman? (Genesis 2:23) ______

Can you picture the tender scene when God first brought woman to man and presented her to him as his wife? Try to imagine the delight God must have felt to see his creation, beautiful and in perfect harmony. No wonder the Scriptures say, "And God saw that it was good. Very good." (Genesis 1:31)

What was the first act God did after creating man and woman? See Genesis 1:28. ______

______

______

What did God commission them to do? ______

______

______

The Hebrew word *ishshah*, similar to *ish* (man), reflects the fact that woman was derived from man (though the word itself may come from a root meaning "to be soft"). What special provision did God make for the man he formed? (Genesis 2:18) ______

______

Who gave woman her name? (Genesis 3:20) ______

What does Eve mean? (Genesis 3:20) ______

Read Genesis 2:10–14 for a glimpse of what must have been an exquisite garden paradise (located in modern-day Iraq). What did God plant in the middle of the garden? (Genesis 2:9) ______

______

What very specific command did God give man? (Genesis 2:16–17) ______

______

In the same verse, what does it say would be the consequence of disobedience? ______

______

What very important work was man to do in the Garden of Eden? (Genesis 2:15, 20) ______

______

______

Once again, what distinguishes man from animals? (Genesis 1:27) ______

______

______

## Discussion Question

How does the creation account differ from theories that suggest that the existence of the universe, the earth, and humanity came into being by another method?

## Personal Application Question

How do you respond to God as your Creator? As your Savior?

Take a few minutes to write a prayer of praise and acknowledgment to God as Creator based on Jeremiah 10:6, 10, 12.

[1]Kapp, Jacob W. "Beginning," *International Standard Bible Encyclopedia.* Edited by James Orr. 1913.
[2]Lindsay, James. "Eternity," *International Standard Bible Encyclopedia.* Edited by James Orr. 1913.

Day Two

# The Tempter Arrives

Now the serpent was more crafty than any beast of the field which the Lord God had made. And he said to the woman, "Indeed, has God said, 'You shall not eat from any tree of the garden'?"
—Genesis 3:1

Scripture teaches the existence of Satan in seven Old Testament books and by every writer of the New Testament.

What was Satan like in his *original* state? Ezekiel 28:12 describes him as "You had the *seal of perfection, full of wisdom and perfect in beauty*" (emphasis mine.) "On the day Satan was created, all the precious stones were prepared" (Ezekiel 28:13, NASB).

What is Satan called in Ezekiel 28:14? ____________________

What is said of him in Ezekiel 28:15? ____________________

____________________

____________________

____________________

*Note:* Ezekiel 28:12–15 describes Satan's unique privileges before his fall and the judgment on him in verses 16–19. Satan was the consummation of perfection in his original wisdom and beauty.

What was his downfall? (1 Timothy 3:6, Isaiah 14:13–14) ____________________

His position in heaven was cast as profane, and he was no longer the covering cherub—his special place of prominence in guarding the throne of God (Ezekiel 28:16). And his name was changed to Satan. God is very concerned with names. Names are personal. Read Psalm 147:4. God numbered and named the ______________________________

Names in the biblical context very often reveal the nature or character of a person and are a means by which we are personally identified. The Lord very often changed the names of people to better suit who they were or what they had become. For example, Genesis 35:10 (NIV) tells us that after Jacob wrestled with the Lord all night, "God said to him, 'Your name is Jacob, but you will no longer be called Jacob; your name will be ____________________________.'"

Matthew 1:21 (NIV) records the greatest name given among men whereby we must be saved. "She will give birth to a son, and you are to give him the name ____________________ because he will save his people from their sins." How majestic is His name!

In Acts 13:9, a sorcerer named Elymas (for that is what his names means) tried to oppose Paul and tried to turn the proconsul from the faith.

In keeping with the changing of names, there are also many personal identifications for the tempter, but for our purposes, we will study only seven of them: Satan, Lucifer, the Devil, the Evil One, the dragon, the deceiver, and serpent. These are not only names for the Devil, but also describe his character. Let's examine them and their use in Scripture in order to get a more complete perspective of exactly who he is, what he does, and his ultimate goal.

The name Satan occurs fifty-four times in forty-seven verses combined in three books of the Old Testament and twelve books of the New Testament.

One of the most familiar uses of this name occurs during a conversation between the Lord and Satan regarding Job. Job 1:6–7 records it as follows: "One day, the angels came to present themselves before the Lord, and Satan also came with them. The Lord said to Satan, 'Where have you come from?' Satan answered the Lord, 'From roaming through the earth and going back and forth in it'" (NIV). (For personal enrichment, read the complete dialogue that continues to Job 2:6.)

When Jesus had fasted forty days, the Devil took Him to a very high mountain and offered to give Him all the kingdoms of the world and their glory if Jesus would fall down and worship him. Read Matthew 4:10 and write the verbal response of Jesus:

________________________________________

________________________________________

________________________________________

What did Paul say Satan did in 1 Thessalonians 2:18? ______________________________

________________________________________________________________________

________________________________________________________________________

The name Lucifer occurs one time in one verse. "How you have fallen from heaven, O Lucifer (literally, *day star*), son of the morning" (Isaiah 14:12, NKJV).

Read Isaiah 14:13–14. In Lucifer's lofty pride, list the five sins (each beginning with the words "I will") that he committed. ______________________________________________

________________________________________________________________________

________________________________________________________________________

________________________________________________________________________

________________________________________________________________________

________________________________________________________________________

*Note:* The five phrases beginning with the words "I will" detail the sins of Lucifer (Satan). He wished to occupy *heaven,* the abode of God Himself. To exalt his throne above the *stars of God* may refer to his desire to rule all the angelic creatures, or it may simply be another way to indicate his self-exaltation. *North,* in pagan literature, indicated the abode of the gods; thus, Satan was ambitious and wished to govern the universe as the council (assembly) of Babylonian gods supposedly did. He wanted the glory that belonged to God alone, and his entire goal was to be *like the Most High.* That is pride at its ugliest!

Devil is used thirty-four times in thirty-two verses in thirteen books of the English Standard Version of the New Testament. Read Ephesians 6:11, and write it here. ______________________

________________________________________________________________________

________________________________________________________________________

"During supper, when the devil had already put it into the heart of Judas Iscariot, Simon's son, to betray him" (John 13:2, ESV).

Read James 4:7. What happens when you resist the devil? ______________________

Evil One captures the essence of the Devil and describes the epitome of who and what he is in just two very descriptive words. It occurs ten times in as many verses in five books of the New Testament in the English Standard Version of the Bible.

"In all circumstances take up the shield of faith, with which you can extinguish all the flaming darts of the evil one" (Ephesians 6:16, ESV).

What do you think is meant by "flaming darts"? ______________________________

______________________________________________________________

Matthew Henry states in his commentary that,

> His temptations are called *darts,* because of their swift and undiscerned flight, and the deep wounds that they give to the soul; *fiery darts,* by way of allusion to the poisonous darts which were wont to inflame the parts which were wounded with them, and therefore were so called, as the serpents with poisonous stings are called fiery serpents. Violent temptations, by which the soul is set on fire of hell, are the darts which Satan shoots at us. Faith is the shield with which we must quench these fiery darts, wherein we should receive them, and so render them ineffectual, that they may not hit us, or at least that they may not hurt us.[1]

"I am writing to you, fathers, because you know him who is from the beginning. I am writing to you, young men, because you have overcome the evil one" (1 John 2:13, ESV).

Dragon is mentioned twelve times in the book of Revelation in the English Standard Version of the Bible. Dragon has all the connotations of a fire-breathing monster, and with a name like Dragon, it does not take much imagination to picture the Devil in your mind's eye.

"His tail swept down a third of the stars of heaven and cast them to the earth. And the dragon stood before the woman (Israel) who was about to give birth, so that when she bore her child (Jesus) he might devour it" (Revelation 12:4, ESV).

"Now war arose in heaven, Michael and his angels were fighting against the dragon. And the dragon and his angels fought back" (Revelation 12:7, ESV).

"And the great dragon was thrown down, that ancient serpent, who is called the devil and Satan, the deceiver of the whole world—he was thrown down to the earth, and his angels were thrown down with him" (Revelation 12:9, ESV).

"And when the dragon saw that he had been thrown down to the earth, he pursued the woman (Israel) who had given birth to the male child (Jesus)" (Revelation 12:13, ESV).

Read the words of Jesus regarding the Deceiver found in John 8:44 (ESV): "You belong to your father, the devil, and you want to carry out your father's desire. He was a murderer from the beginning, not holding to the truth, for there is no truth in him. When he lies, he speaks his native language, for he is a liar and the father of lies."

"For many deceivers have gone out into the world, those who do not confess the coming of Jesus Christ in the flesh. Such a one is the deceiver and the antichrist" (2 John 1:7, ESV).

"Then I heard a loud voice in heaven, saying, 'Now the salvation, and the power, and the kingdom of our God and the authority of His Christ have come, for the accuser of our brethren has been thrown down; he who accuses them before our God day and night'" (Revelation 12:10, ESV).

What are two activities of Satan found in Revelation 12:9–10? ______________________________

____________________________________________________________________________

____________________________________________________________________________

Since Satan is the deceiver and accuser, who is Jesus according to John 14:6? ______________

____________________________________________________________________________

____________________________________________________________________________

Write 1 Timothy 2:5. ____________________________________________________________

____________________________________________________________________________

How does this verse and verse 6 describe who Jesus is and what He has done? ____________

____________________________________________________________________________

____________________________________________________________________________

Do you see two extremes? Satan is the deceiver; Jesus is the mediator. Satan is the accuser; Jesus is the ransom.

Serpent is used to refer to Satan ten times in ten verses in three books of the New International Version of the Bible.

"Now the serpent was more crafty than any of the wild animals the LORD God had made. He said to the woman, 'Did God really say, You must not eat from any tree in the garden'?" (Genesis 3:1, NIV)

"But I am afraid that just as Eve was deceived by the serpent's cunning, our minds may somehow be led astray from our sincere and pure devotion to Christ" (2 Corinthians 11:3, NIV).

Think of a time when you were deceived. What was the result of your deception?

____________________________________________________________________________

____________________________________________________________________________

____________________________________________________________________________

____________________________________________________________________________

As a quick review, list the evil activities of Satan stated in the following verses:

Genesis 3:4 ______________________________

Matthew 4:3 ______________________________

Luke 8:12 ______________________________

John 8:44 ______________________________

John 13:2 ______________________________

Acts 13:10 ______________________________

2 Timothy 2:26 ______________________________

Hebrews 2:14 ______________________________

1 Peter 5:8 ______________________________

Jude 1:9 ______________________________

Revelation 12:9 ______________________________

Does it not seem ironic that this same Devil appeared in the first book of Scripture as well as the last book? Through the eyes of Scripture, we witness the fact that Satan derives his greatest satisfaction with rendering death and destruction. The name Serpent takes us back to the beginning of today's lesson, when the tempter arrived in the garden. In tomorrow's lesson, we will see trouble in the garden.

## Discussion Question

What is the difference between *pride* and *humility*? (For example, who is elevated in pride? Who is elevated in humility?)

## Personal Application Question

Do you recognize pride in your own life? Why should we combat pride? See Isaiah 42:8 and Isaiah 45:5

Take a few minutes to write a prayer that glorifies God for His immeasurable grace.

[1]Henry, Matthew. *Matthew Henry's Commentary on the Whole Bible* (New York: Fleming H. Revel, Co., n.d.)

## Day Three

# Trouble in the Garden

Do not be deceived, God is not mocked; for whatever a man sows, that he will also reap.
—Galatians 6:7 (NKJV)

Satan is introduced in Genesis 3:1 as ________________. Now the serpent that Satan used was apparently a beautiful creature in its uncursed state. Whether Satan took the form of a serpent or actually possessed the serpent is not clear. In yesterday's lesson, we learned that the serpent was more ____________________________________________
than any other beast of the field (Genesis 3:1). *Crafty* means clever—not in a degrading sense at this point. And because Satan is crafty, he comes in the disguise for whatever fits his purpose.

Satan evidently found his perfect opportunity to tempt Eve. She and her husband may have been walking together in the garden and passed near the tree in the midst of the garden. Maybe Eve stopped to admire its beauty while Adam was occupied a short distance away. The Scriptures do not detail this for us, but we can gather from the account of the temptation that this very easily could have been the situation with Eve. We do know that Satan did not *bring* her to the forbidden tree as he brought Christ to a high pinnacle of the temple and to a high mountain in order to tempt Him (Matthew 4:5, 8, NASB).

What was the first action Satan took? _____________________________ The serpent began a theological conversation with Eve, and God and His words were the subject. Satan was planting his own garden in Eve's mind—casting seeds of doubt as to whether God really meant what He said.

The tempter never called out, "Come, I'll teach you to sin." If he tempted us in such a manner, we would immediately recognize his strategy and flee, would we not? But remember, a whisper of deception hides behind every temptation!

Do you wonder how Satan knew God's command to Adam and Eve when He forbid them to eat from a certain tree in the garden? See Ezekiel 28:13. Where was Satan? ____________________

______________________________________________________________

Notice how Satan cleverly worded his question to Eve in Genesis 3:1. Write his words. __________

______________________________________________________________

______________________________________________________________

What do you think Satan was trying to imply about God—that He was unfair or restrictive? That God makes false threats? Write your thoughts. ______________________________

______________________________________________________________

______________________________________________________________

How did Eve respond? (Genesis 3:2–3) ______________________________

______________________________________________________________

According to Eve's words, from which tree were Adam and Eve commanded not to eat? _________

______________________________________________________________

It is clear that Eve understood God's command. What would be the consequence of disobedience? _ ____________________ Again, Eve's own words revealed her clear understanding of disobeying God's command.

In Genesis 3:4, we watch Satan boldly contradict God when he says, "You surely shall not die." We see the crafty one trying to usurp God's authority. Satan took it upon himself to explain God's purpose in forbidding them to eat from that one tree. Read Genesis 3:5. How did Satan explain God's reason for forbidding them to eat the fruit of the forbidden tree? ______________________________

______________________________________________________________

______________________________________________________________

Eve still remained in her perfect innocence and purity before yielding to temptation.

Read Genesis 3:6. Can you picture Satan quietly observing from a nearby place as Eve gazed at the luscious fruit, wondering what it would taste like, contemplating in her mind what it would be like to be as wise as God, thinking God would not know? Who knows how long she stood there twisting strands of hair around her finger, considering. We can only speculate the dilemma going on in her mind—*Should I or shouldn't I? It looks so good. How can anything that looks so good be bad? I really want this! Why shouldn't I have it?* And Eve picked the fruit from the tree!

Where was Eve's focus—herself or God? ____________________

How does your focus affect your awareness of whether or not you are flirting with temptation? ____

____________________

____________________

____________________

What kinds of reasoning, arguments, or justifications do you come up with when faced with a temptation you may be seriously considering? ____________________

____________________

____________________

Which of the three categories of the sins of self-deception found in 1 John 2:16 do you think Eve was guilty of?

_______lust of the flesh
_______lust of the eyes
_______pride of life
_______all of the above

Write 1 John 2:17. ____________________

____________________

Do you recognize self-deception—something you reason as justifiable to sway your decision to yield to temptation? Give an example of what you might consider to be self-deceptive reasoning for your own defense in your personal experience. ____________________

____________________

____________________

____________________

Eve was guilty of pride and lust. Satan appealed to her desire for the best in life and encouraged her to choose against her understanding of truth with tragic consequences.

Genesis 3:6 says, "She took from its fruit and ate, and she ______

______

______

Satan tempted Eve so that by her, he might tempt Adam; he tempted Job by his wife and Christ by Peter. Satan often sends temptations by unsuspected hands—those who have the most interest in and influence upon us.

Satan already knew there would be dire consequences for himself for rebelling against God again, but he was willing to bear them in order to bring death to the man and woman. If Satan could not rule over the angels, the heavens, the universe in all their glory, he could at least spoil God's creation in its perfect state and bring death and ruin. Satan is the destroyer, and he is most appeased when he destroys.

We've already established that Adam heard God's direct command not to eat from the fruit of the tree of knowledge of good and evil, which was in the middle of the garden, but he ate anyway. Adam was guilty of deliberate disobedience and rebellion against God.

So far in this lesson, we have witnessed Satan's sin of pride and rebellion and Eve's addition to the mix with self-deception and lust. Then Adam threw into the caldron his disobedience and rebellion. Mankind fell, and great was its fall—and we are only on Genesis 3!

Genesis 2:9 indicates there may have been two trees in the midst of the garden from which Adam and Eve were forbidden to eat. Name the two trees. ______

______

______

______

If our first couple would have eaten from the tree of life as well as the tree of the knowledge of good and evil, man would have lived in his sinful state forever separated from fellowship with God.

Read Proverbs 4:14–15. What do these verses say we should do regarding the path of the wicked and the way of evil men? ______

______

______

______

Write James 4:7. ______

______

Eve did not hold the advantage of having the *written* Word of God to guide her, and we don't have the audible command from the mouth of God to direct us. So who do you think has the greater advantage—Eve or us? ______________________ Why? ______________________

______________________________________________

______________________________________________

______________________________________________

Jeremiah 17:9 says, "The heart is deceitful above all things and beyond cure. Who can understand it?" (NIV) This verse describes the condition of natural man. We are all prone to sin. Romans 3:10 says it plainly: "There is no one righteous, not even one" (NIV). The choices we make are far-reaching and may have dire consequences, and if left to ourselves, we would choose evil every time. But thanks be to God, who gives us the victory through our Lord Jesus Christ. (1 Corinthians 15:57, NASB)

## Discussion Question

What does Eve's experience teach us about the far-reaching consequences of our choices—either through our own self-deception or through the lies of the deceiver?

Do the far-reaching consequences of our choices teach us that "no-fault" choices were *illusions* for Adam and Eve then and still are for you and me today? There is no one to blame. Are we held accountable for the choices that we make? Are there always consequences with choices (good or bad)?

## Personal Application Question

Recall the hurtful times when the tempter won in your life. What strategy did he use? Did he use the same method over again?

Take a few minutes to write a prayer asking God to show you areas of *self-deception* and *outside temptation* so He can lead you to the truth in His Word to overcome evil.

Day Four

# Dire Consequences

Therefore, just as sin entered the world through one man, and death through sin, and in this way death came to all men, because all sinned.
—Romans 5:12 (NIV)

Yesterday's lesson ended with Eve succumbing to temptation, taking the forbidden fruit, eating it, and then giving it to her husband. Do you wonder if that first bite was sweet, juicy, and delicious, inviting our couple to take more? Or do you think that before the sweet juice trickled down their throats, they felt the keen sense of guilt and shame?

Whatever the scenario, it was not just a matter of spitting the evidence from their mouths. Genesis 3:7 says, "Then the eyes of both of them were opened, and they knew that they were naked."

Did you ever have a dream that you were running down your high school hallway naked and couldn't find your locker or some similar dream? Do you remember how glad you were when you woke up and realized that it was just a bad dream? Well, there was no waking up from a bad dream for Adam and Eve. The reality was immediate. They had sinned!

Read Genesis 3:8. Who did Adam and Eve hear? ______________________ What was He doing? ___________________ During what part of the day did this happen? ______________________ What did Adam and Eve do? ________________________________ Where did they try to hide? __________________________ "Quick, hide!" they must have whispered to each other, scurrying behind a tree. But can you imagine trying to run from God with no place to hide? Think of a time in your own life where you may have tried to hide from God. It's a scary situation to be in, isn't it?

After enjoying perfect fellowship with the Lord God in an exquisitely beautiful and peaceful garden, describe the reason you think Adam and Eve must have felt that made them try to hide themselves from their Creator. ______________________________

______________________________

Squirming in their skin would not begin to describe the feeling; don't you agree? What did the Lord God say? (Genesis 3:9) ______________________________

What did the man answer? (Genesis 3:10) ______________________________

______________________________

We now know they felt not only guilt and shame, but also fear! Why did they feel fear? (Genesis 3:10)

______________________________

______________________________

When a child gets caught with a hand in the cookie jar, the first emotion he or she may feel is fear. Of what? Being caught? Being punished? How about when an adult gets found out in a lie; what is the first emotion he or she may feel? Fear? Guilt? Shame? Dread? Embarrassment? Of these very uncomfortable emotions, do you agree that fear may be the one that causes the adrenaline to rush through our entire being with the most unpleasant effects of all?

The Lord did not ask, "Why did you disobey me?" or "Why are you here in the middle of the garden?" What two questions did He ask? (Genesis 3:11) ______________________________

______________________________

______________________________

______________________________

Suddenly, as Adam and Eve stood before the Lord, they realized that the Lord God knew of their disobedience. There was no covering it up. There was no denying it. There was no excuse—although they did try to make excuses. Instead of answering the Lord's question directly, what did the man say? (Genesis 3:12) ______________________________

______________________________

How do you think Adam felt toward God when God first brought him his beautiful wife in Genesis 2:22? ______________________________

We now see that Adam blamed God for "the woman whom Thou gavest to be with me." Adam also blamed Eve: "She gave me from the tree, and I ate" (Genesis 3:12, NASB).

Eve was surely not about to take the blame. What was her response when the Lord asked her what it was that she had done? (Genesis 3:13) ______________________________________________

______________________________________________

Evidently, the serpent was still lingering around the forbidden tree—maybe even feeling smug that God's perfect couple was no longer innocent. But the blame buck stops here. Satan was the first to receive God's curse.

Suddenly the middle of the Garden of Eden became a courtroom, and God was the righteous judge! Read Genesis 3:14. There was no defense, advocate, or leniency. Satan was cursed more than all cattle and every beast and made to slither on his belly; dust would be his nourishment.

The sentence passed upon the tempter may be considered as lighting upon the serpent, the brute-creature that Satan made use of that was, as the rest, made for the service of man but was now abused and hurt. Therefore, to testify displeasure against sin and jealousy for the injured honor of Adam and Eve, God fastened a curse and reproach upon the serpent. The Devil's instruments must share in the Devil's punishments. See here how God hates sin and especially how displeased He is with those who entice others into sin. The Devil's crime was that he tempted Eve to eat that which she should not; his punishment was that he was necessitated to eat that which he would not: "Dust thou shalt eat."[1]

To the woman, God said, "I will greatly increase your pains in childbearing; with pain you will give birth to children. Yet, your desire will be for your husband, and he will rule over you" (Genesis 3:16, NASB).

Here the two-fold sentence is passed upon the woman for her sin: pain in child-bearing would be greatly multiplied. "And your husband shall rule over you." Headship of the husband and submission by the wife were ordained by God as part of the creation order. (See Ephesians 5:23) "And yet," the Lord continues, "your desire shall be for your husband." The word *desire* can also mean "an attempt to usurp or control" as in Genesis 4:7 that speaks of sin crouching at the door *and its desire is for you...* Thus it may be stated this way: You will now have a tendency to dominate your husband, and he will have the tendency to act as a tyrant over you. Beloved, apart from restoration of mutual respect and dignity through Jesus Christ, the battle of the sexes would never end!
Read Genesis 3:17. In your own words, write what God said to Adam regarding his punishment: __

______________________________________________

Man is condemned to hard labor in order to make a living; whether in the fields or some other form of labor, man must work hard. "By the sweat of your face you shall eat bread." (Genesis 3:19, NASV)
Even the ground is cursed. In what way is the ground cursed? (Genesis 3:18)________________
What act of grace and mercy did God do for Adam and Eve? (Genesis 3:21)________________

______________________________________________

Read Genesis 3:22–24. What did God do in order to prevent Adam and Eve from also eating of the tree of life? ______________________________

______________________________

Driving the man and his wife from the garden was both a punishment and an act of mercy lest they should eat of the tree of life and live forever in a state of alienation from God.

Let's look at some of the other ramifications of sin and how it spread. Adam and Eve had two sons, Cain and Abel. In the course of time, both young men brought their offerings to the Lord. Cain offered fruit of the ground, and Abel offered the firstlings of his flock. Cain had an attitude of unbelief, whereas Abel had a true heart. When Cain saw that the Lord accepted Abel's offering and not his, he became jealous of his brother. Read Genesis 4:8. What did Cain do? ______________________________

______________________________

______________________________

Immediately, the Lord confronted Cain. Read Genesis 4:9–13 to see the dialogue between the Lord and Cain and Cain's punishment.

More than a thousand years passed, and then we come to Genesis 6:5–6, 11–12. What do these verses record? ______________________________

______________________________

______________________________

______________________________

______________________________

The earth became so vile with sins too numerous to list that God caused a flood to destroy every living creature and all the vegetation except eight people, two of every species of animals, and flying birds. These were saved on the ark.

Thousands of years have passed since the flood, and man has continued his spiral downfall into sin and depravity. Take, for instance, the sacrificing of children by fire to the false god Molech as recorded in Leviticus 18:21 and 2 Kings 16:3, 23:10. We have to ask ourselves, "Are we any different today with the more than fifty million abortions of innocent babies from the 1970s through 2012?"

We may think of idolatry as the worshipping of idols—a pagan act done by those in remote jungles or in the eastern religions where the worship of the statue of Buddha or some other object is practiced. But idolatry can be used as a broad term to denote the worship by one who is a slave to the depraved ideas his idols (whatever they may be) represent and are referred to as lusts—lusts of the flesh, lusts of the eyes, and the pride of life.

Idolatry, in Greek, is *eidololatria.* In English, idolatry (from *eidolon* and *latreia,* "service") is found in 1 Corinthians 6:9, Galatians 5:19–21, Colossians 3:5, and in the plural, in 1 Peter 4:3.[2]
Heathen sacrifices were sacrificed to demons (1 Corinthians 10:19); there was a dire reality in the cup and table of demons and in the involved communion with demons. In Romans 1:22–25, idolatry, the sin of the mind against God, and immorality, sins of the flesh (Ephesians 2:3) are associated with and traced to the lack of acknowledgment of God and of gratitude to Him. An idolater is a slave to the depraved ideas his idols represent (Galatians 4:8–9) and thereby to diverse lusts (Titus 3:3).[2]
"You will suffer the penalty for your lewdness and bear the consequences of your sins of idolatry. Then you will know that I am the Sovereign LORD" (Ezekiel 23:49, NIV).

The acts of the sinful nature are obvious: sexual immorality, impurity, and debauchery; idolatry and witchcraft; hatred, discord, jealousy, fits of rage, selfish ambition, dissensions, factions and envy; drunkenness, orgies, and the like (Galatians 5:19-20, NIV).

"Put to death, therefore, whatever belongs to your earthly nature: sexual immorality, impurity, lust, evil desires and greed, which is idolatry" (Colossians 3:5, NIV).

"For you have spent enough time in the past doing what pagans choose to do—living in debauchery, lust, drunkenness, orgies, carousing and detestable idolatries" (1 Peter 4:3, NIV).

If it were left to man, we would all be doomed! But do not despair! We are not a people without hope! "For God so loved the world that He gave His only begotten Son that whoever believes in Him should not perish, but have everlasting life" (John 3:16, NKJV).

## Discussion Question

If you had been in the Garden of Eden and the tempter spoke to you in pleasant tones, do you think you would have done anything differently? Be honest. How do you think you would have responded?

## Personal Application Question

What are ways you strive to make right choices and keep yourself aware of the consequences of bad choices?

Take a few minutes to write a prayer, asking God to show you areas of sin that may need to be confessed. Keep in mind that "If we say that we have no sin, we are deceiving ourselves, and the truth is not in us. If we confess our sins, He is faithful and righteous to forgive us our sins and to cleanse us from all unrighteousness" (1 John 1:8–9, NASB).

Tomorrow, we will be encouraged to see God's great love for us, the grace and mercy He gives, and the promised hope of peace through Jesus Christ.

[1]Henry, Matthew. *Matthew Henry's Commentary on the Whole Bible* (New York: Fleming H. Revell, Co., n.d.)
[2]Vine, W. E. "Idolatry", *Vine's Expository Dictionary of New Testament Words*. 1940.

Day Five

# Promised Savior

We all, like sheep, have gone astray, each of us has turned to his own way;
and the LORD has laid on him the iniquity of us all.
—Isaiah 53:6 (NIV)

> As the echo of the crunching of the fruit was still sounding in the garden, Jesus was leaving for Calvary. 1
> —Max Lucado

How God's heart must have grieved! How His indignation and wrath must have been set ablaze! But in spite of sin, His unconditional love never wavered. How could it? It is God's very nature to love. Write 1 John 4:16.

God is love, yes; but God is also holy and righteous and cannot just ignore sin.

God's desire to have fellowship with those created in His own image must have intensified, for He had already purposed a most unimaginable plan! This plan was a plan like no other—unfathomable in its scope, unprecedented in its purpose, unmatched in its wisdom, and unstoppable in its accomplishment.

The Lord God Almighty would send His only Son into His own creation. This Son would be born in the likeness of man except without sin to take the wrath of God upon Himself in our place for our sins. Jesus, Son of God and Son of Man, became the *visible glory of God!*

In Paul's letter to the Philippians, Paul summed it up with words plain in text but profound in meaning. Paul wrote,

> Have this mind among yourselves, which is yours in Christ Jesus, who, though He was in the form of God, did not count equality with God a thing to be grasped (exploited), but made himself nothing, taking the form of a servant, being born in the likeness of men. And being found in human form, He humbled Himself by becoming obedient to the point of death, even death on a cross. (Philippians 2:5–8, ESV)

We may ask, *Why? For what purpose did Jesus have to shed His blood on the cross?* We find the answer in Hebrews. Write Hebrews 9:22. ______________________________

______________________________

Isaiah recorded God's words in Isaiah 46:9–10 (ESV). "Remember the former things of old; for I am God, and there is no other; I am God, and there is none like me, declaring the end from the beginning and from ancient times things not yet done, saying, 'My counsel shall stand, and *I will accomplish all my purpose*'" (emphasis mine). So what was God's purpose for Jesus having to shed His blood? His blood was shed for the ______________________________.

"Oh, the depth of the riches both of the wisdom and knowledge of God! How unsearchable are His judgments and unfathomable His ways. For who has known the mind of the Lord, or who became His counselor?" (Romans 11:33–34, NASB)

Write 1 Timothy 2:5–6. There is one ______________________________

______________________________

______________________________

Who is this mediator/man? ______________________________Jesus gave ______________________________ as a ______________________________

Some people, in their quest to gain heaven, may put their confidence or even their faith in a priest, their own good works, their church, their family background, their ability to keep the Ten Commandments, their knowledge of God, or a host of other means to try to gain salvation.

God's standard, apart from Jesus Christ, is perfection. "Be perfect, therefore, as your heavenly Father is perfect" (Matthew 5:48, NIV). And perfection, apart from Jesus Christ, is impossible for man to attain. Who could attain a standard of perfection high enough to be acceptable to the God who is holy, holy, holy? As it is written, "There is no one righteous, not even one; all have turned away, they have together become worthless; there is no one who does good, *not even one*." (Romans 3:10, 12, NIV, emphasis mine). Before faith in Jesus, where did you place your hope for going to heaven? ___

______________________________________________

______________________________________________

As a child, I attended a Lutheran parochial grade school for eight years. We had memory verses to recite every morning, songs to learn for choir, prayers to say before lunch, etc. I certainly knew there was a God, but whether Jesus as Savior was taught, I do not know. It may have been taught, and I may not have heard the words. At any rate, I was confirmed not knowing to what I was making affirmation. Through my teen years, I developed a fear of God, of death, and even of living. Even though I had many fears, I still thought that because I knew about God, I would go to heaven. You may have had a similar background, or your background may be at the other end of the spectrum. Briefly describe your childhood background. ______________________

______________________________________________

______________________________________________

______________________________________________

______________________________________________

______________________________________________

______________________________________________

Having head knowledge of God is good, but is that enough for salvation? ______________

What does God say? Write Isaiah 43:11. ______________________________

______________________________________________

Also write Isaiah 43:25. ______________________________________

______________________________________________

______________________________________________

______________________________________________

One commentator says, "He *will not remember* the sin, which intimates not only that he will remit the punishment of what is past, but that it shall be no diminution to his love for the future. *When God forgives he forgets.* What is the grounds and reason of the pardon? It is not for the sake of anything in us, but for his own sake, for his mercies'-sake, his promise-sake, and especially for his Son's sake, and that he may himself be glorified in it."[2]

Paul wrote of this good news of forgiveness of sins in 2 Corinthians 5:21, where he said, "He made Him who knew no sin to be sin on our behalf that we might become the righteousness of God in Him" (NASB). We are made right with God.

Read Romans 8:1. There is therefore ______________________________ for those who are in ______________________________.

Write 2 Corinthians 5:17. ______________________________
______________________________
______________________________

There are abiding results of the new life in Christ.

Under the law of the Old Testament, the priest, in elaborate sacrifices several times a year, would offer the blood of unblemished lambs and goats for the covering of the sins of the people. However, in the New Testament, Christ appeared as our high priest; more amazingly, Christ also was the sacrifice to take away our sins. When John, the baptizer, saw Jesus coming toward him at the Jordan River, he said, "Look, the *Lamb* of God, who *takes away* the sin of the world!" (John 1:29, NIV, emphasis mine)

That's what God purposed when He sent His only begotten Son into the world so that whoever believes in Him should not perish, but have eternal life (John 3:16). This was done once for all—one sacrifice, one time, for all sins, for all time. This truth is confirmed again in Hebrews 9:26 (NIV): "But now he has appeared once for all at the end of the ages to do away with sin by the sacrifice of himself."

When I was thirty years of age, my childhood friend told me how she came to know the difference between *knowing about* God and His Son Jesus Christ and *knowing* God and Jesus as Savior. For the first time since grade school, all the Bible verses that I had memorized came into focus. The head knowledge that I had learned integrated into my heart, where faith began to sprout, grow, and flourish. How about you? Do you remember a time when your head knowledge became a matter of the heart? Write how you came to *know* Jesus. ______________________________
______________________________
______________________________
______________________________
______________________________
______________________________
______________________________
______________________________

As extraordinary as the death of Jesus, Son of God and Son of Man, may be, His resurrection was His crowning glory. Peter, a disciple of Jesus and an eyewitness of His resurrection, spoke these words: "Seeing what was ahead, he spoke of the resurrection of the Christ, that he was not abandoned to the grave, nor did his body see decay" (Acts 2:31, NIV). Again, Acts 4:33 (NIV) says, "With great power the apostles continued to testify to the resurrection of the Lord Jesus, and much grace was upon them all."

Imagine a possible dialogue between the apostle Peter and Paul when Paul went up to Jerusalem to become acquainted with Peter and stayed with him fifteen days (Galatians 1:18).

Paul: How long had you been a disciple of Jesus?
Peter: 'Bout three years.
Paul: Must have been great to walk with Him all that time!
Peter: Great is a small word to describe it.
Paul: What's the greatest thing you saw the Lord Jesus do?
Peter: Aside from raising Lazarus from the dead, His own resurrection was profound!
Paul: Any doubts that Jesus is the Christ?
Peter: Not anymore.

Review Romans 8:1. One more time now, who has no condemnation? ____________________
______________________________________________ Why is this true? See 2 Corinthians 5:17.
________________________________________________________________________________
________________________________________________________________________________

## Discussion Question

Genesis 3:21 says that the Lord God made garments to cover the nakedness of Adam and Eve. What do you think is the significance of this act? What does it say about the fellowship between God and man, and what is the reason it is recorded in Scripture? (Keep in mind that when the first couple sinned, the first thing they realized was that they were naked, and they tried to hide.)

## Personal Application Question

Since grace is getting what we don't deserve (John 1:16) and mercy is not getting what we do deserve (Titus 3:5), how does faith figure in? (Acts 20:21, Ephesians 2:8)

Take a few minutes to write a prayer, giving thanks to the Father for sending His Son into the world that through Him we might be saved. If you do not know Jesus as Lord and Savior, why not ask Him now?

[1]Lucado, Max. *And the Angels were Silent.* (Oregon: Multnomah Publishers, 1992), 25.

[2]Henry, Matthew. *Matthew Henry's Commentary on the Whole Bible* (New York: Fleming H. Revell, Co., n.d.)

# Week Two
# GOD'S COVENANT

Day One
**Background And Culture**

Day Two
**The Call of Abraham**

Day Three
**Sarah's Impatience**

Day Four
**Consequences**

Day Five
**Learning Through Consequences**

## Day One

# BACKGROUND AND CULTURE

But I will establish My covenant with you.
—Genesis 6:18

Today, we will start our journey through distance and time from the Garden of Eden to a land more spacious and fertile than it is beautiful. We are going to Canaan to visit with Sarah, Abraham's wife. But, before we meet with Sarah, please allow me to review some familiar history and background.

After Adam and Eve were banished from their garden home and the angel with the flaming sword stood guard at the entrance, the Garden of Eden, which at one time captivated the essence of God's created beauty, became uninhabited and overgrown with weeds. It became symbolic of man's depraved and sinful condition.

Gen. 6:5-6 says, "Then the LORD saw that the wickedness of man was great on the earth, and that every intent of the thoughts of his heart was only evil continually. And the LORD was *sorry* that He had made man on the earth, and He was *grieved* in His heart." *Sorry* means that *God felt just and holy displeasure against sin and sinners.*

God would destroy the earth and all it contained with a flood. But Noah found favor with God and was spared. God's covenant is first mentioned in Gen. 6:18. With whom did God first make a covenant? ____ Who were the only people spared in the catastrophic flood that would destroy every living thing and all vegetation on the earth? See Gen. 6:8, 18 ______________________________

______________________________________________________________________

______________________________________________________________________

We have no way of knowing for certain, but if there are no gaps in the chronology of mankind as listed in Gen. 5, almost 2000 years elapsed between creation and the time of the flood.

After the flood, the three sons of Noah who came out of the ark were: (Gen. 9:18) ______________, ____________________, and ______________________ and from these the whole earth was populated. The descendants of Japheth settled in the area that stretched across Eurasia from the Black and Caspian Seas to Spain. The descendants of Ham went to Africa and later spread west along the Mediterranean coast of N. Africa.

The descendants of Shem originally settled in the area north of the Persian Gulf, but eventually settled in Ur in southern Mesopotamia which is 220 miles SE of modern day Baghdad, Iraq. Noah blessed Shem saying, "Blessed be the LORD, the God of Shem; and let Canaan be his servant." (Gen. 9:26, NASB) Yahweh will be Shem's God and Shem's blessing. Jews are of Semitic (Shem) descent and since they are the ancestors of Abraham, we will concentrate on this line of Noah's descendants; *the line receiving the call of God to be His chosen people.* A selective list of ten generations from the time of the flood to Abraham is recorded for the purpose of tracing the lineage of Noah's son, Shem, down to Abraham. (Gen. 11:10-26)

Tomorrow we will meet Abraham and his wife Sarah and note how God's covenant is renewed with Abraham. We will spend most of our time with Sarah, however, as we continue our journey through Old Testament times meeting various women, learning from their decisions and reflecting on our own responses to similar situations. We will also dig deeply to unearth more treasures in God's Word.

What was God's command found in Gen. 9:1? ______________________________

______________________________________________________________________

Read Gen. 11:4 and note that the people built a city to *prevent* the spread of people throughout the earth in direct defiance of God's command. All the people spoke the same language and worked to build a tower as a symbol of their achievements. How did God thwart man's plans as found in Gen. 11:7? ______________________________________________________________

And so the Lord scattered the people over the face of the whole earth. What was the name of the tower according to Gen. 11:9? ______________________________________________

## Discussion Question:

Read Gen. 11:6 and discuss what other possibilities man may have been trying to accomplish by building a tower whose top will *reach into heaven.*

## Personal Application Question:

Would you rather have recognition for an accomplishment you achieved *or* would you rather be an "unknown" who is known to be obedient to God's commands. Explain.

Take a few minutes to write a prayer asking God to give you a heart to praise Him for who He is and a will to do what He commands.

Pack your satchels, ladies. Tomorrow we will meet with Abraham and Sarah and will travel with them as they set out on their journey that will take them into unimaginable situations.

## *Notes*

Day Two

# THE CALL OF ABRAHAM

I will make you a great nation and I will bless you.
—Genesis 12:2

Ten generations after the flood, Abram was born in 2165 B.C. His name means "exalted father," the progenitor of God's chosen people who were first called Hebrews; two generations later, they were called the people of Israel and then they became known as Jews. Later, Abram's name was changed to Abraham. Abraham was married to the woman we plan to spend time with this week. Originally, her name was Sarai, but was later changed to Sarah, and for the remainder of this week's study, we will refer to Abram and Sarai as Abraham and Sarah.

Early in their marriage, Abraham and Sarah lived with Abraham's father, Terah, and his nephew, Lot, in Ur among the Chaldeans. Now the Chaldeans were a wealthy, sophisticated, and pagan people. According to Joshua 26:2, Abraham's father, Terah, also served other gods. In other words, he worshipped idols, so we can safely assume that Abraham did likewise.

It was from this background and culture and after the death of Abraham's father, that God called Abraham to come out from among this people to a land which He would show him; a rich and fertile land called Canaan. Can you imagine what Sarah must have felt when Abraham told her that the LORD appeared to him and said to take with him his wife and his nephew and all their flocks and herds and go to this strange new land? What do you think would have been your first question to Abraham if you were Sarah? ______________________________

______________________________

What else did the LORD say to Abraham? Write Gen. 12:2 ______________________________

______________________________________________________________________

______________________________________________________________________

How old was Abraham when he set out for Canaan? Gen. 12:4 ____________________

While in route to Canaan, the LORD appeared again to Abraham declaring that He would give all this land to Abraham's *descendants*. It was at this time that Abraham began to call on the name of the LORD.

As Abraham, Sarah, and Lot with their flocks and herds journeyed on toward the Negev, a severe famine in the land forced Abraham and his company to detour to Egypt. As they neared Egypt, Abraham asked Sarah to do a preposterous thing.

We must understand the culture of the time, or what Abraham asked of Sarah would seem too ludicrous for her to even consider. In Egypt, marriage was highly respected and to take another man's wife was strictly forbidden. However, if the husband was killed, that would make the widow fair game for Pharaoh to take as his wife and to do as he pleased with her. Abraham told Sarah plainly, "They will kill me, but they will let you live." So when Abraham asked Sarah to say to the Egyptian officials that she was his *sister* rather than to admit she was actually his wife, she quietly obliged. What do you think you would have done if you were in that situation? ______________________

______________________________________________________________________

______________________________________________________________________

But Abraham's deception involved him in the one difficulty he hoped to escape. The king's courtiers saw the handsome Hebrew woman, and extolled her beauty before Pharaoh. He summoned her to the apartments of the palace, and captivated by her loveliness, he determined to make her his wife. During the agonizing hours of suspense for Abraham, and the concealed anguish of Sarah in her conscious degradation, the time wore heavily away, until the judgments of God upon the royal household brought deliverance. Pharaoh, though an idolater, knew by this supernatural infliction upon him, that there was guilt in the transaction, and called Abraham to an account. (Gen 12:18) He had nothing to say in self-acquittal, and with a strange magnanimity, was sent away quietly with his wife and his property; followed only by the reproaches of Pharaoh, and his own wakeful conscience. (Gen 12:15-19)

Even though Sarah was 65 years old at this time, what did Pharaoh's officials do when they saw Sarah? (Gen. 12:15) ______________________________________________________

How was Abraham treated? (Gen. 12:16) ______________________________________

Who protected Sarah from becoming defiled? (Gen. 12:17)______________________________

As a direct result, Abraham and Sarah were promptly escorted out of Egypt, but Abraham was allowed to keep the extravagant gifts of flocks and herds, and male and female servants. In addition to the livestock and servants, Abraham also had much gold and silver. He was a very rich man and Lot also, so to travel with such a vast company of livestock and servants was no small feat. After all, there was no boarding the livestock into box cars and shipping them to their destination. They had to drive the herds and flocks and to make sure the livestock had food and water along the way. They had to set up their tents and take down their tents whenever they stopped for the night. They cooked out in the open and had to be on guard constantly against predators for themselves as well as for their livestock.

Because the land could not support the vast herds of Abraham and Lot, they separated. Lot chose the valley of the Jordan and Abraham settled in the land of Canaan. In your own words, write what the LORD said to Abraham? (Gen. 13:14-17) ______________________________________

______________________________________________________________________

When Abraham told Sarah that the Lord would bless him and make his descendants as numerous as the dust of the earth, do you suppose she had the faintest curiosity as to how this was going to happen? After all, she had never borne any children to Abraham because of her infertility and she was well beyond child-bearing years. All this left Sarah with little hope and much desperation to conceive.

Maybe your struggle is not with infertility. Perhaps it is a struggle of a different nature, but nonetheless, a desperate longing that only God can fulfill. Whatever the struggle, God cares deeply and uses the difficulty to evoke from us the response that He is seeking for our good. See Prov. 3:5-6

Notice that the LORD sought out Abraham; Abraham did not seek the LORD. What do you think is the significance of this? ______________________________________________________

______________________________________________________________________

Does this not ring true for each of us? The Father calls us to His Son. Read Romans 1:7, 8:28; 1 Corinthians 1:9, 24; and 1 Peter 2:9, 5:10

Let's take a look at Abraham's qualifications that he should be called by God to be the one from whom God would make a great nation; a nation with people too numerous to count; a nation with a king who was said to have a heart after God's own heart; a nation from which the Savior of the world would come!

So far, we have seen that Abraham's father was an idol worshipper; Abraham also served other gods, he lived among a pagan people, he was a nomad, he was rich, and he was married to Sarah who was barren.

Abraham did not seem to have very impressive credentials, wouldn't you agree? So what was it about Abraham that God should call him into covenant; that he would bless him with descendants too numerous to count; that in him all the families of the earth should be blessed? Before we discover why, let's go back to the first covenant God made with man. What was the covenant that God made with Noah? See Genesis 9:11, 15 ____________________

____________________

What was the sign of His covenant? Genesis 9:13 ____________________

What was the blessing Noah pronounced upon Shem? Genesis 9:26 ____________________

____________________

From the line of which son of Noah was Abraham a descendant? (Gen. 11:10-26) __________
Who instituted the Covenant with Abraham? (Gen. 12:1-4; 17:2, 7) ____________________

Stephen, before he was stoned, said, "Hear me, brethren and fathers! The God of glory appeared to our father Abraham when he was in Mesopotamia, before he lived in Haran, and said to him, "Depart from your county, you and your relatives, and come into the land that I will show you." (Acts 7:2-3) What was Abraham's *response* to God's call?
(Gen. 12:4; Heb. 11:8) ____________________

Abraham may not have had impressive qualifications, but he had a heart to believe and a mind to obey and in God's eyes, it was counted as righteousness.

What was the sign of this covenant God made with Abraham? (Gen. 17:10-11)__________

____________________

What did Abraham do? (Gen. 15:6; Rom. 4:3) ____________________

Let's look at Sarah's qualifications that she should be the mother of this great nation. Sarah was a Hebrew maiden of remarkable beauty with dark luminous eyes and dark hair. She had a quiet strength, and graceful dignity. She was not one to go unnoticed. Surely she must have captured the admiration of the Chaldean shepherds, wouldn't you agree?

Not only was Sarah beautiful, she was submissive to her husband. This was shown when she agreed with him to say to Pharaoh's officials that she was Abraham's sister. She was 65 years old and she was barren. Do you think one's beauty or one's submissive spirit qualifies one to be called of God for such an amazing role in God's plan and purpose? ____________________ Explain.

____________________

____________________

Think about your own qualifications. Which of your characteristics might make you worthy to be called of God to be His child? ___

Apart from Jesus Christ, I cannot think of <u>any</u> qualities that would make me worthy to be called by God either.

What about Jesus? Let's look at His credentials. Read Hebrews 1:2-4 and list nine qualities that are said about Jesus that cannot be said about man.

1. ___
2. ___
3. ___
4. ___
5. ___
6. ___
7. ___
8. ___
9. ___

Jesus is the *radiance* of His glory which means effulgence or flood of resplendent light. The word means an *outshining*, not a reflection. NKJV uses the word *brightness.*

Verse 4 says that "He has inherited a more excellent name than the angels."
Read Phil. 2:9-11 and write a one-sentence summary of these verses. ___

___

___

Do not give up hope for Sarah. Or for yourself. Ever!

## Discussion Question:

In our first week's study, we learned about temptation and in this week's study, we come face to face with trials. Discuss the difference between temptation and trials.

## Personal Application Question:

I would rather have God-ordained trials in my life than to be in the crosshairs of Satan's temptations, wouldn't you? Tell of a *trial* and a *temptation* you experienced noting the effects of each and the lesson learned.

Take a few minutes to write a prayer asking for faith and strength to sustain you when trials and temptations assail you.

Tomorrow, we will be on the move again as we will put ourselves in Sarah's sandals. We may stand aghast, we may be filled with empathy, we may feel her desperation, we may cry for justice. For certain, the cords of emotion will be pulled in many different directions.

Day Three

# SARAH'S IMPATIENCE

Count the stars if you are able … so shall your descendants be.

—Genesis 15:5

## Canaan

Ten years had passed from the time the LORD made a covenant with Abraham to bless him with descendants as numerous as the dust of the earth. Then the word of the LORD came to Abraham in a vision. "Your reward shall be very great." (Gen. 15:1, NASB) Abraham asked the LORD if his servant, Eliezer of Damascus, would be his heir since he had no children, but that was not to be. Are you beginning to feel Abraham's perplexity yet? How then, LORD? When?

Think of a time when you were certain of a promise of the Lord that seemed would never materialize. How did you respond?

______Perseverance in unwavering faith?
______Doubt?
______Impatience?
______Taking matters into your own hands?
______Give up?
______Other?

How did the LORD respond to Abraham's question? See Gen. 15:4 ______________________

______________________________________________

______________________________________________

Not only did the LORD say that Abraham's heir would be his own offspring, but that his descendants would be as many as the stars in the sky and who could count the stars?
With this added assurance, Abraham ______________________________ (Gen. 15:6).
Write Rom. 4:3 ______________________________________

______________________________________________

______________________________________________

Now let's see how Sarah handled the situation. Read Genesis. 16:2. What was Sarah's solution to their childlessness? ______________________________________

This maidservant is Hagar – her *Egyptian* maid! Hagar was among the many female and male servants Pharaoh had given to Abraham when they had journeyed to Egypt during the famine as we learned in yesterday's lesson. Hagar had no choice in the matter since she was a slave to her mistress; albeit Hagar was an educated and cultured woman of Egypt, but still the maidservant to the wife of a herdsman. Today, we would call Hagar a surrogate mother, but Sarah had no other means of obtaining a child through Hagar except to give her maidservant to her husband. That was a desperate measure to the core, wouldn't you say? (It always is when we try to tip the hand of God in our favor.)

Do you empathize with Sarah? ____________ Why or why not? ____________________

______________________________________________________________

Do you have compassion for Hagar? _________ Why or why not? ____________________

______________________________________________________________

Do you identify with Abraham in his plight? ________ Why or why not? ______________

______________________________________________________________

We just read that Abraham believed God, but Genesis 16:2 says "Abraham listened to her." And why not? After all, He was 85 years old and this seemed like the only plausible plan. Abraham would still be the father since the blessing was to be to his descendants, which eliminated his servant Eliezer. So he consented -- with disastrous results!

Read Isaiah 64:4

How many times do we run ahead of the Lord thinking that we have come up with the perfect plan. This reminds me of the time very early in my Christian walk when my friend and I came up with what we considered to be the perfect plan that just had to ensure her husband's salvation. Bob was flying to Florida on a business trip so Carol and I prayed that the Lord would have Bob sit next to a Christian man. For three hours, Bob would listen to the Gospel. He had to. He was on a plane with no other seats available. By the time they reached Florida, Bob would be a Christian. Simple. Straightforward. Why wouldn't it work? Surely, God would use our plan, wouldn't He?

Think of a time when you devised a plan that seemed right and would certainly receive God's approval only to prove the complete opposite. Briefly write of such a time. ____________________

______________________________________________________________

______________________________________________________________

______________________________________________________________

Of course, neither Carol nor I had taken to heart Isaiah 64:4 or Psalm 27:14 or Psalm 130:5 or Lamentations 3:26. What is the main theme of these verses? ____________________

______________________________________________________________

Why was our plan destined for failure? ______________________________________

______________________________________________________________

Why was Sarah's plan destined for failure as well? ______________________________

______________________________________________________________

On the plane, Bob sat next to a man all right. But this man could hardly wait to get to Florida and out of his wife's sight to do every sort of mischief he could think of. When Bob called Carol to tell her of his safe arrival, he said, "You are not going to believe who I sat next to on the plane!"

Carol, of course, was expecting to hear that he had put his trust in Jesus as Lord and Savior, but, alas, quite the opposite!

"He was *pure evil*," Bob said. (I know, sometimes we put words together that are opposites, but sometimes they work.) It was this realization of evil in the flesh and his own sinful nature that eventually turned Bob to the Lord; conviction of the Holy Spirit as it is called. Carol and I realized that our plan would not have had the impact or maybe even the lasting effect that the Lord's plan had; not only on Bob, but also on Carol and myself.

## Discussion Question:

The Bible says that we shall receive whatever we wish. Read John 15:7. What is the stipulation in this verse? What danger do we risk if we think we can ask for anything we wish for and expect to receive it without abiding in Jesus?

Discuss what it means to *abide* in Jesus? (With reference to state or condition: to remain as one, not to become another or different)

## Personal Application Question:

How do answered prayers glorify the Father? (Jn. 15:7-8; Matt. 5:16) What is the key to answered prayer and producing fruit?

Take a few minutes to write a prayer asking the Lord to direct all your ways and to guide all your steps that you may abide in Him to the glory of the Father.

Satan's Plan is to destroy:

**Doubt** – Makes you question God's Word and His goodness

**Discouragement** – makes you look at your problems rather than at God

**Diversion** – Makes the wrong things seem attractive so that you will want them more than the right things

**Defeat** – Makes you feel like a failure so that you don't even try

**Delay** – Makes you put off doing something so that it never gets done

# ...CES

...ore Me and be blameless.

...is 17:1

A...

...eaction toward her mistress, Sarah? (Genesis 16:4) ___

___

Sa... Hagar to her former status as a slave, though we may s... r would no longer be Abraham's concubine (Genesis

...Abraham loved his son and named him Ishmael, which means ...ntention, hatred, bitterness, and jealousy between Sarah and her ...is hands in the air and said to Sarah, "She's your maidservant; do ...s 16:6) And so she did!

...mily member with whom you have unsettled contention. Maybe this ... up silently at family gatherings year after year. Maybe all those phone ... essing things with that special friend have stopped. What if that person who is pr... from you called and asked for forgiveness? What would you do? ___

___

___

What if you were the one to make that phone call or personal visit? How do you think the other person would react? ___

___

Write James 2:8. ______________________________

______________________________

______________________________

For many years, Sarah made life so miserable with her harsh treatment towards Hagar that Hagar and her teenage son, Ishmael, fled into the wilderness—presumably to go back to her native land, Egypt. Before we become too critical of either woman, however, let's take a look at how the entire scene played out.

One day, as Hagar sat weeping as her young son lay dying of thirst in the wilderness, the Lord appeared to Hagar. He comforted her, provided water for her and her son, and then blessed her with these words: "I will greatly multiply your descendants so that they shall be too many to count" (Genesis 16:10). How did Hagar respond to the Lord? (Genesis 16:13) ______________________________

______________________________

______________________________

The Lord also told Hagar to return to her mistress and submit herself to Sarah. Do you think Hagar obeyed? See Genesis 17:23–25, 21:9. ______________________________

*Side note:* The descendants of Ishmael are Arabs, and since they claim Abraham as their ancestral father, the well-known and volatile hostility between Arabs and Jews has continued for centuries. Jews, however, are the descendants of promise—the people of God's covenant He made with Abraham (Genesis 17:7).

When Abraham was ninety-nine years old, the Lord appeared to him again and said that He would bless Sarah and give Abraham a son by her; she would be a mother of nations, and kings of peoples would come from her. What did Abraham do when he heard these words? (Genesis 17:17)__________

______________________________

Some feel that Abraham laughed for joy, but verse 18 indicates it was an expression of doubt as he struggled to match his faith to his circumstance. Have you ever struggled to keep the faith amidst contrary circumstances? Explain your answer. ______________________________

______________________________

______________________________

______________________________

Abraham asked if Ishmael might be the promised heir of blessings. What did God reply? Write Genesis 17:19. ______________________________

______________________________

______________________________

______________________________

What provision did God make for Ishmael? (Genesis 17:20) ______________________________

______________________________________________________________________

______________________________________________________________________

With whom will God establish His covenant? (Genesis 17:21) ____________________________

What was the sign of the covenant God made with Abraham? (Genesis 17:10) _______________

______________________________________________________________________

Did Abraham perform what was commanded him by God in keeping the covenant? See Genesis 17:23. ______________________________________________________________

One day, as Sarah stayed in the shade of their tent and Abraham sat at the tent door, he saw three men approach along the dusty road and stand opposite him in the shade of the oak trees. Abraham ran out and greeted them in the customary way, bowing low before them and offering water so that they could wash their hot, dusty feet. Who was one of the three men? (Genesis 18:1) ___________ The other two men were angels.

As the men conversed, Sarah listened unobtrusively from the tent. Abraham offered the three strangers bread and meat to eat. As Sarah prepared the cakes, she heard one of the men ask Abraham, "Where is Sarah, your wife?" (Genesis 18:9)

Abraham answered, "She is in the tent." Do you think hearing the man refer to her by name may have caught her breath a little? Do you think she may have pressed her ear closer to the tent door, since she recognized that these were more than just three strangers passing by? These men were on a mission!

Then Sarah heard the man say, "I will surely return to you at this time next year, and behold, Sarah, your wife, shall have a son." The promise may have been made to Abraham, but it most definitely was meant for Sarah's ears as well, wouldn't you say? Keep in mind that the Lord had told Abraham that he was to name his son Isaac a year prior to his birth.

In the privacy of her tent, Sarah did what you and I would probably have done if we were in the tent instead of Sarah. She laughed to herself. The absurdity of such a statement—that she should have a son! She was eighty-nine years old and would be ninety when her son would be born if it were true! *How ludicrous! How preposterous!*

But then she heard the man say, "Is anything too difficult for the Lord?" When she heard those words, a trickle of hope began to infiltrate her soul, much like melting snow of early spring drips off a roof and seeps into the soil. Think of a time when you had lost all expectation in a particular situation but then you clung to a glimmer of hope. Was your faith restored? Write your experience.___________

For what purpose did God choose Abraham? (Genesis 18:18) ___________

God would bring about His promise so that all the nations of the earth would be blessed through Abraham. How does this blessing pertain to us? (Galatians 3:8–9) ___________

Does everyone receive this blessing? If not, who then receives this blessing? (Galatians 3:7)

What is this blessing that reached beyond the Jewish people to all the nations of the earth? Is it not salvation? "I am not ashamed of the gospel, because it is the power of God for the salvation of everyone who believes: first for the Jew, then for the Gentile" (Romans 1:16, NIV).

According to this verse, who receives this salvation? ___________
Are you counted among the believers? ___________

## Discussion Question

Why is it important that people don't put their trust in good works for salvation? See Ephesians 2:8–9.

## Personal Application Question

Do you have saving faith in Jesus Christ? ___________ If so, how did you come to have this saving faith?

Take a few minutes and write a prayer of thanksgiving for your salvation.

Our lives are brimming with times when we must make choices. Some choices have dire consequences, and others just have effects. Tomorrow, we will see the importance of *learning* from the consequences that result from the decisions and choices we make. Life is a time of learning; making choices is part of the process. Be encouraged. You are not alone.

## Day Five

# Learning through Consequences

From of old no one has heard or perceived by the ear, no eye has seen a God besides you, who acts for those who wait for Him.
—Isaiah 64:4 (ESV)

When time passes without answers to prayers, we may be tempted to take matters into our own hands. We know God answers prayer; it's another thing to wait for Him. Waiting is hard; believing while waiting is harder still. What does Psalm 27:14 say? ______________________

______________________________________________________________________

______________________________________________________________________

Write Psalm 130:5. ______________________________________________________

______________________________________________________________________

In this week's study, we learn that God made the promise to Abraham and Sarah that He would bless the whole world through the son He would give them. At first, they waited eagerly. As time dragged on, their anticipation turned to disappointment, their disappointment to discouragement, their discouragement to doubt, their doubt to disbelief, and their disbelief to disobedience. This spiral always takes this progression, but the good news is that we can choose to disembark this train before we involve ourselves in the consequences of the pending train wreck that is sure to follow.

Several other sons promised by God would bring a blessing to the parents, the nation of Israel, and the whole world. We will mention a few here. Name these sons and their callings.
Exodus 3:4, 10 ______________________________________________________
Joshua 1:1–2 ______________________________________________________

1 Samuel 1:20, 3: ____________________

1 Samuel 16:12–13 ____________________

Luke 1:13–14, 17 ____________________

Luke 1:31–33, Matthew 1:21 ____________________

After two decades of waiting for the promised son, Sarah took matters into her own hands. At what point did she regret her decision, and what were the results? (Genesis 16:1–5) ____________________

When circumstances became unbearable for Hagar, what decision did she make that nearly cost her son's life? (Genesis 16:6) ____________________

Had the Lord not intervened, surely Hagar and Ishmael would have died in the wilderness. Have you ever made a decision that might have caused irreparable harm had the Lord not intervened? Describe such a time. ____________________

When faced with a seemingly impossible situation, what did Sarah (as well as each of us) need to learn about the Lord? (Genesis 18:14, Luke 1:37) ____________________

Psalm 86:5–7 ____________________

Proverbs 3:5–6 ____________________

Matthew 19:26 ____________________

Complete this sentence of Galatians 3:1: "The righteous shall live by ____________________."

Abraham believed God, and it was reckoned to him as righteousness (Galatians 3:6). The just—those who are justified—will be justified by faith. That is why the law cannot justify us. It cannot make us righteous. And the law is not of faith (Galatians 3:12). The law is of works. "The law says, but the man that doeth them shall live by them" (Galatians 3:12). The law places the emphasis upon the doing—the obedience—where "*faith places the emphasis upon trusting in God*" (emphasis mine). According to this, who are the righteous? ____________________

In what areas do you need encouragement?

_______ Waiting patiently

_______ Persevering in prayer

_______ Trusting

_______ Believing

_______ Other

When waiting for answered prayer seems endless, what action are you mostly likely to take?

_______ Pray

_______ Take control

_______ Give up

_______ Become angry

_______ Keep on keeping on

_______ Other

When the Lord said that Sarah would conceive and bear a son, what did Sarah do while still inside the tent? Genesis 18:12 ________________________________________________

Is God's knowledge of your private thoughts, doubts, fears, and actions a comfort or a distress to you? Explain. ________________________________________________

________________________________________________

________________________________________________

When the Lord questioned Sarah about her action, what did Sarah do? (Genesis 18:15) _________

________________________________________________

Why? ________________________________________________

Why did Adam and Eve try to hide from God after their sin? (Genesis 3:10) _______________

________________________________________________

________________________________________________

Have you ever experienced fear as a result of sin? ____________ Explain. _______________

________________________________________________

________________________________________________

How should we deal with our sin? (1 John 1:9) ______________________________

Psalm 46:10 says, "Be still and know that I am God" (NIV). What does that verse mean to you? __

________________________________________________

________________________________________________

The following year, Sarah did conceive and did bear a son, just like the man had said outside their tent. Abraham and Sarah named him Isaac. Sarah was very protective of their son—especially against the taunts from Ishmael, which only heightened the contention between Sarah and Hagar, forcing Hagar to flee once again with Ishmael.

Ishmael grew and lived in the wilderness and became an archer. Then Hagar took a wife for Ishmael from the land of Egypt (Genesis 21:20–21).

## Discussion Question

According to Isaiah 53:10, what satisfies the wrath of God against sin?
______ Our good works
______ Christ's death on the cross
______ Keeping the Ten Commandments
______ Hiding from God
______ Lying to God

According to Hebrews 9:22, what is necessary for the forgiveness of sin?
______ Our good works
______ The shedding of Christ's blood
______ Keeping the Ten Commandments
______ Hiding from God
______ Lying to God

According to Acts 16:31 and Romans 10:9, what do we need to do to have salvation? Check all that apply.

______Nothing
______ Believe
______ Trust
______ Repent
______ Do good works
______ Attend church
______ Confess sins
______ Read the Bible
______ Obey God

## Personal Application Question

If you could see your prayer life from God's perspective, would that change the way you pray? If so, how?

Take a few minutes to look up several of your favorite Bible verses on patience, and rather than just reading them, pray them. No Word of God shall be void of power, so arm yourself with His might when you pray. Example: "Father in heaven, I have need of endurance so that when I have done Your will, I may receive what is promised. May it never be that I would throw away my confidence for lack of patience, but that I would put my hope in You and wait patiently upon You" (Hebrews 10:35–36).[1]

## *Notes*

[1]Kroon, Rita. *Praying the Scriptures* (Denver, Colorado: Outskirts Press, 2011), 41.

# Week Three
# Contrived Blessings

Day One
**Background and Culture**

Day Two
**Rebekah—The Perfect Match**

Day Three
**Managing or Manipulating?**

Day Four
**Deceitfulness—The Ultimate Insecurity**

Day Five
**Deceit and its Consequences**

## Day One

# Background and Culture

Do not fear, for I am with you.
—Genesis 26:24

Yesterday, we bid farewell to Sarah in Hebron in the land of Canaan. But before we take our leave of our elderly friend, let's see what happened with her beloved son, Isaac.

God tested Abraham in a most unusual way. What did God tell Abraham to do?
See Genesis 22:2. ______________________________________________

______________________________________________

______________________________________________

God does not tempt anyone with evil, as James pointed out in James 1:13. To *tempt* is to test, try, prove, or solicit to *evil.* James 1:2 says, "Consider it all joy, my brethren, when you encounter various trials," and James 1:12 says, "Blessed is the man who perseveres under trial; for once he is approved, he will receive the crown of life, which the Lord has promised to those who love Him." The same Greek word is used to mean "trials that are designed to prove the quality of one's character." We can be confident that God was ________________ Abraham and not ____________________ him.

Human sacrifice was practiced (though not by the godly) in Old Testament times, and Abraham would have been acquainted with it in Mesopotamia. God's intention here was not to see if Abraham loved God more than he loved Isaac since God already knew that he did, but to test Abraham's faith whether Abraham believed God's promise concerning his descendants.

We never have to fear being tempted (to solicit evil) by God. We can be certain that all temptations come from either Satan or ourselves. See James 1:14.

I am fairly confident that Sarah did not know about this venture with Abraham, Isaac, and the servant. Even in her old age, I can imagine she would have trekked alongside of Isaac to make sure he would be safe. Don't you agree?

Write the words of Isaac found in Genesis 22:7. ______________________________

______________________________________________________________

Can you picture a father hearing those words from his innocent young son? They must have torn Abraham's heart nearly in two. But what did Abraham answer? (Genesis 22:8)

______________________________________________________________

______________________________________________________________

Abraham built the altar and arranged the wood. He bound his son and laid him on the altar. Have you ever been tested to what you felt were the outer limits of your faith? Explain. ____________

______________________________________________________________

______________________________________________________________

______________________________________________________________

______________________________________________________________

______________________________________________________________

But that is what God does; He stretches our faith like the skin of a drum so that our faith may increase. What does the testing of our faith produce? (James 1:3)______________________
"And if endurance has its perfect result, we are made _____________ and __________ lacking in _________________." *Perfect* here does not mean "without sin" but rather "whole, complete."

As Abraham stretched out his hand and took the knife to slay his son, the angel of the Lord called, "Abraham! Abraham! Do not stretch out your hand against the lad, and do nothing to him; for now I know that you fear God, since you have not withheld your son, your only son, from Me." Because God knows all things, does it not make sense that this testing was for Abraham's benefit and maybe even for Isaac's benefit as well? Nothing was more important to Abraham than his trust and obedience to God. What an example Abraham set for his son!

How about you? Is the evidence of your faith enough to be an encouragement or a detriment to others?

______________________________________________________________

______________________________________________________________

God provided the sacrificial lamb for the burnt offering. Abraham raised his eyes and saw a ram caught in a thicket behind him, and Abraham offered the ram in place of his son.

This is a beautiful picture of God providing the sacrificial Lamb that would be sacrificed in our place for our sins. "For God so loved the world that He gave His only begotten Son that whoever believes in Him should not perish, but have eternal life" (John 3:16, NASB).

Write John 1:29. ______________________________________________

______________________________________________

What blessing did God give to Abraham because of his obedience? (Genesis 22:16–18)

______________________________________________

______________________________________________

______________________________________________

Write Galatians 3:9. ______________________________________________

______________________________________________

Sarah and Abraham certainly must have discussed the customary marriage arrangements for their son, Isaac. They surely did not want their son to marry any of the daughters of the Canaanites but someone from Abraham's own people in Mesopotamia over five hundred miles from Palestine.

Sarah, however, did not live to meet her daughter-in-law but died with the confidence that God would bless Isaac with descendants too numerous to count.

Tomorrow, we will follow our guide to a new land as we continue our journey. We will see firsthand that the ends do not justify the means, regardless of the reasons used for such actions. I am very glad to have you along!

## Discussion Question

What would be the most difficult thing or person for you to give up?

Why?

## Personal Application Question

Did you identify with Sarah or her circumstances in any way? If so, write it and relate it to your own life along with the end results of the choices you made.

Take a few minutes to write a prayer asking that your measure of faith would be a blessing to a sister sojourner.

## Day Two

# Rebekah—The Perfect Match

He will send His angel before you, and you will take a wife for my son from there.
—Genesis 24:7

When Abraham was well advanced in years, he had one more mission to accomplish. He had to find a wife for his son, Isaac. He no longer had Sarah by his side, but to honor her desires for their cherished son, he sent his trusted servant to find a wife from his people in Mesopotamia over five hundred miles away. Are you ready to meet her? Then mount your camel, and let us be on our way.

Traveling to another country with a camel caravan was in itself no small feat. However, for his master's sake, the faithful servant made the trip. After the servant arrived and made the camels kneel down by the well outside the city, what is the next thing the servant did? (Genesis 24:12) ____________

______________________________________________________________________

How did this servant specifically pray to the God of Abraham? (Genesis 24:13–14)____________

______________________________________________________________________

______________________________________________________________________

When was the servant's prayer answered? (Genesis 24:15)______________________________

______________________________________________________ Isn't that amazing!

Do you pray specifically, or are your prayers said using general terms? ______________

______________________________________________________________________

Which prayers are easier for us to recognize as being answered directly? _______________

______________________________________________________________________

Why is it important to recognize answered prayers? ______________________________

______________________________________________________________________

"I offer You, O most high God, a sacrifice of thanksgiving. I will honor Your name. I will give thanks to You, Lord, for You are good and Your loving kindness is everlasting" (Psalm 50:23, 118:29).[1]

When the servant asked for a drink, how did Rebekah respond? (Genesis 24:19–20)____________

______________________________________________________________________

Was the servant's prayer answered? ______________________________

What did the servant do? (Genesis 24:26, 48) ______________________________

Why did the servant worship and bless the Lord? (Genesis 24:48)____________________

______________________________________________________________________

How is the girl, Rebekah, described? (Genesis 24:16)______________________________

______________________________________________________________________

Genesis 24:21 says that "the man was gazing at her in silence." What do you suppose he was wondering? ______________________________

Who arranged this match? (Genesis 24:7)______________________________

Do you see the sovereign hand of God moving to accomplish His purpose? Can you glimpse, perhaps in hindsight, when you recognized that God was moving on your behalf to accomplish His purpose? Explain. ______________________________

______________________________________________________________________

Why travel to Mesopotamia? (Genesis 24:3–4) ______________________________

______________________________________________________________________

What did Rebekah do when the servant presented her with a gold ring weighing a half shekel and two gold bracelets weighing ten shekels? (Genesis 24:28) (At that time, a shekel was a weight of perhaps half an ounce.)______________________________

______________________________________________________________________

These gifts were expensive, and Rebekah certainly recognized them as such. Do you think Rebekah realized what this meant for her? Why or why not? ______________________________

______________________________________________________________________

Such expensive gifts to the bride-to-be and her family constituted a kind of dowry, assuring the financial competence of the groom.

Rebekah's father was named Bethuel. Bethuel was Abraham's nephew—the son of Abraham's brother, Nahor (Genesis 11:27, 29; 24:15). Her brother was Laban. (Keep this name in the back of your mind, because we will see the significance of Laban later in our study.) But for now, we see that Bethuel and Laban saw that this was from the Lord and agreed to the marriage of our beautiful Rebekah (Genesis 24:50), but ultimately, the decision would be Rebekah's.

What did the servant present to Rebekah? (Genesis 24:53)____________________
What gifts did the servant give to Rebekah's brother and mother?____________________

The following morning, Rebekah's mother and brother had second thoughts about Rebekah's leaving so soon and tried bargaining with the servant. "Let the girl stay with us a few days, say ten; afterwards she may go" (Genesis 24:55). Think of a situation in which you tried to buy some time from either a person or from the Lord. Explain. ____________________

In God's economy, there is a time to wait and a time to act. This was a time for action. See Genesis 24:56. The servant knew his master would expect him home with expediency. He had business to do at home; therefore, as one that preferred his work before his pleasure, he was for hastening home.[2]

Finally, someone decided to ask our dear Rebekah if she would return with the servant. What did her mother and her brother say? (Genesis 24:57)____________________

What was Rebekah's response? (Genesis 24:58) ____________________

Rebekah's family sent her, along with her maids, on their way with the servant and his men, knowing they would more than likely never see their beloved daughter and sister again. What were their final words to Rebekah? (Genesis 24:60) ____________________

What was God's promise to Abraham regarding Sarah in Genesis 17:16? ____________________

Isaac went out to meditate in the quietness and solitude of the field. It was toward evening. As he walked along, perhaps he speculated whether the servant had success in finding his perfect match.

Maybe he was contemplating the death of his mother, Sarah, and feeling the loss of not having his mother there to meet his bride or to see her grandchildren. Maybe he was anticipating the return of the servant and was eager to see what kind of woman would have such confidence and determination that she would travel over five hundred miles to marry a man she had never met. Could he possibly have wondered if the woman would even have agreed to come at all to marry him?

As he walked along a furrow, he looked up and saw a caravan of camels approaching. He quickened his step to meet them.

Rebekah lifted up her eyes and saw a man in the field coming toward them. When she saw the man, she dismounted from her camel and asked the servant, "Who is that man walking in the field to meet us?" The servant answered, "He is my master." Surely her heart must have beat a little faster when she realized she was about to meet the man who would become her husband!

Rebekah behaved herself very becomingly when she met Isaac; understanding who he was, she "alighted off her camel" (Genesis 24:64) and "took a veil, and covered herself" (Genesis 24:65) as a token of humility, modesty, and subjection.[3]

"He guides the humble in what is right and teaches them his way" (Psalm 25:9, NIV).
"Be completely humble and gentle; be patient, bearing with one another in love" (Ephesians 4:2, NIV).
"God opposes the proud but gives grace to the humble" (1 Peter 5:5, NIV).

Rebekah almost seems shy, wouldn't you agree? She certainly exhibited *humility, modesty,* and *subjection*—all qualities that make a beautiful woman even more desirable to her husband. Would you rather be known for your physical beauty or your inner beauty? ______________________
Why? ______________________________________________________________________

______________________________________________________________________________

As they walked along, Rebekah listened as the servant recanted to Isaac the details of the events of the previous few weeks, including the blessing given to Rebekah by her family upon their departure. Isaac must have felt even more certain that the promise of becoming a great nation that God had made to his father, Abraham, would certainly be realized through him.

How old was Isaac when he made Rebekah his wife? (Genesis 25:20) ______________________

Genesis 25:5 says that Abraham gave all that he had to Isaac, but to the sons of his concubines, he gave gifts (probably starter flocks and herds) and sent them away from Isaac. Abraham provided for all his children, but he made Isaac his principal heir—his only son of promise. It is interesting to note that when Abraham died at age 175, Isaac and Ishmael buried him in the cave with Sarah (Genesis 25:9). The presence of Ishmael at Abraham's funeral shows reconciliation between him and Isaac.

Think of your own family or friends. Is there a reconciliation that has been ignored for too many years? What if you were the one who initiated the reconciliation? What if you were the one to forgive, even if the other person did not admit his or her fault? What if you were the one who took Ephesians 4:32 to heart? "Be kind and compassionate to one another, forgiving each other, just as in Christ God forgave you."

Who blessed Isaac after Abraham's death? (Genesis 25:11) ______________________________

## Discussion Question

What does Ephesians 4:32 mean when it says to be *kind* and *compassionate*; forgiving each other?

## Personal Application Question

What does it mean to you to *grieve the Holy Spirit?* (Ephesians 4:30)

Take a few minutes to write a prayer based on Luke 6:36–37.

Tomorrow we will spend time with Rebekah after twenty years of marriage. She loved Isaac and was loyal to him, but what would she do when she was faced with a heart-wrenching decision?

[1]Kroon, Rita. *Praying the Scriptures* (Denver, Colorado: Outskirts Press, 2011), 14.
[2]Henry, Matthew. *Matthew Henry's Commentary on the Whole Bible* (New York: Fleming H. Revell, Co., n.d.)
[3]Henry, Matthew. *Matthew Henry's Commentary on the Whole Bible* (New York: Fleming H. Revell, Co., n.d.)

## Day Three

# Managing or Manipulating?

I will bless you, and multiply your descendants, for the sake of My servant Abraham.
—Genesis 26:24

After traveling through distance and time, it is good to rest in the company of our hostess, Rebekah. Twenty years passed since Isaac received his beautiful bride, and Isaac and Rebekah still loved and respected one another. Life was good, except for one smudge—they had no children.

Genesis 25:21 says, "Isaac prayed to the Lord on behalf of his wife." Why? ____________________

______________________________________________________________________

This certainly was not the only time he had prayed to have a son, wouldn't you agree?

Then Rebekah conceived twins! But she had such a struggle within her womb that she inquired of the Lord as to what this could mean. What explanation did the Lord give Rebekah? (Genesis 25:23)

______________________________________________________________________

______________________________________________________________________

This struggle within Rebekah's womb foreshadowed the struggle between the two peoples (the Edomites and the Israelites) of which the twin boys were the progenitors. The younger would occupy the preeminent place that normally went to the firstborn.

When the boys were born, the first one born was red and hairy all over, like he was wearing a garment. Isaac and Rebekah named him Esau. His name anticipates the play on the meaning of Esau's other name, Edom. Afterward, his brother was born with his hand holding onto Esau's heel, and they named him Jacob, which means "heel catcher" or "trickster."

When the boys grew up, Esau was a skilled hunter—an outdoorsman. Jacob was a peaceful man—amiable, pious, and cultured. Isaac loved Esau, because Isaac had a taste for wild game, but Rebekah loved Jacob.

Was there rivalry among the siblings in your family? Did your parents have favorites? What sorts of tension did this add to your family dynamics?____________________

________________________________________

________________________________________

Read James 2:9. Write it here. ____________________

________________________________________

Read Acts 10:34, Deuteronomy 10:17, and 2 Chronicles 19:7. What is the common theme of these verses?____________________

Let's listen as Rebekah tells us of an incident between her two sons that sets the smoldering coals of deceit ablaze with lifelong consequences.

> One day, Jacob had cooked some stew when Esau came in from hunting in the field. Esau was famished and asked for a bowl of stew. But Jacob said, *"First sell me your birthright."* (Genesis 25:31) I stood there not believing what I heard; not daring to breathe. But Jacob looked steadily at his brother; holding a bowl of steaming stew just out of Esau's reach. Then Esau said, "I am about to die of hunger so of what use then is the birthright to me?" I could not believe my ears. Without even flinching, Jacob said, "First swear to me." So Esau swore to him and sold his birthright to Jacob and Jacob gave his brother a bowl of the lentil stew.
>
> Esau proved his proverbial impetuous nature once again and Jacob showed a side of himself that I had only glimpsed these past twenty years. I told Jacob not to say anything to his father how Esau had sold his birthright and that I would handle the situation if it should arise with his father.[1]

Do you think Rebekah was managing or manipulating at this point? Explain. ____________________

________________________________________

________________________________________

Think honestly about your own situations in your family, at school, at work, among friends, or in relationships. Have you ever been a manipulator or one who has been manipulated? What feelings did manipulation evoke in you? ______________________________

______________________________

A birthright of the eldest son gave him precedence over his brothers and assured him a double share of his father's inheritance. Let's look ahead to other Scriptures regarding the birthright. Deuteronomy 21:17 says, "But he shall acknowledge the first-born, the son of the unloved, by giving him a double portion of all that he has, for he is the beginning of his strength; to him belongs the right of the first-born." It could be forfeited by committing a serious sin, as was the case in 1 Chronicles 5:1, which says, "Now the sons of Reuben the first-born of Israel (for he was the first-born, but because he defiled his father's bed, his birthright was given to the sons of Joseph, the son of Israel; so that he is not enrolled in the genealogy according to the birthright." The birthright could also be bartered, as it was in the instance of Esau. Whatever the reason, the one forfeiting his birthright displayed a despising of his birthright and was not taken lightly.

To add to the family woes, Esau married two heathen women—additional evidence of his spiritual dullness. These two daughters-in-law brought grief to both Rebekah and Isaac. See Genesis 26:35.

## Discussion Question

What command is given to husbands in Ephesians 5:28? ______________________________

______________________________

What command is given to wives in Ephesians 5:33? ______________________________

______________________________

How are children to treat their parents according to Ephesians 6:1? ______________________________

______________________________

What further command is given fathers in Ephesians 6:4? ______________________________

______________________________

How does showing favoritism provoke children to anger? ______________________________

______________________________

## Personal Application Question

Has sibling rivalry or parent favoritism in your extended family had a lasting effect on you? ______ Explain.

Do you find yourself struggling with favoritism in your immediate family? ____________
What are the consequences?

Take a few minutes to write a prayer on the royal law found in James 2:8.

Tomorrow we will spend a time of turmoil with Rebekah. Be strong and encouraged.

[1] Kroon, Rita. *Letters from the Past* (Denver, Colorado: Outskirts Press, 2011), 26.

## Day Four

# Deceitfulness—The Ultimate Insecurity

Bless me, even me also, O my father!
—Genesis 27:34

We saw Rebekah and her family begin to unravel, come apart at the seams, and become fractured from disunity. Today we will witness the progression of true family dysfunction. You may feel actions are justified. You may feel empathy. You may be alarmed that people can be capable of such deception. Or you may realize with deep gratitude *that but for the grace of God, there go I.*

What promise did God make to Isaac? (Genesis 26:24)________________________________

____________________________________________________________

For whose sake did God appear to Isaac with such a promise? ________________________

Though the covenant made with Abraham was initiated by God's unconditional grace, God delighted to acknowledge the worthiness of Abraham and to confirm the covenant to Isaac.

The Bible does not tell us the relationship between the twin brothers after Esau sold his birthright to Jacob for a bowl of lentil stew—only that "Esau ate and drank, and rose and went on his way." (Genesis 25:34) We can only surmise that the brothers led separate lives, but how they interacted with each other is left in the silent pages of history.

Many years passed since that incident. Isaac was nearly blind physically, but he may also have been blind to the fact that Esau had bartered his birthright because he was hungry and that he married heathen women out of rebellion. Nevertheless, Isaac still favored Esau, and Rebekah still favored Jacob.

Rebekah overheard Isaac say to Esau, "I am old and I do not know the day of my death. Now then, please take your gear, your quiver, and your bow, and go out to the field and hunt game for me; and prepare a savory dish for me such as I love, and bring it to me that I may eat, so that I may bless you before I die" (Genesis 27:3–4).

A blessing is different than a birthright. A *blessing* is the handing over of legal power, which is more valuable than any amount of goods or property given in the birthright. A blessing was something that fathers gave to each of their sons. Receiving the blessing meant being the head of the clan—having all the power to make decisions for the entire tribe.

What was Rebekah doing? (Genesis 27:5) ______________________________

What did Rebekah do with what she heard? (Genesis 27:6)______________________
Who came up with a plan? (Genesis 27:8) ______________________________
What was Rebekah's plan? (Genesis 27:9–10)____________________________
______________________________________________________________
______________________________________________________________

What was Jacob's concern? (Genesis 27:11–12) __________________________
______________________________________________________________

How did Rebekah convince Jacob? (Genesis 27:13)_________________________
______________________________________________________________

Why do you think Rebekah perpetrated this deception against Isaac?

_______She reasoned to herself that Jacob would ensure the survival of the clan, whereas Esau could very likely sell out to someone for whatever present need he may have had at the time.
_______She favored Jacob so much that she could not bear to have Esau receive the blessing.
_______Rebekah had a better chance of being cared for by Jacob than Esau.
_______She resented Esau for bartering away his birthright and felt that he did not deserve the blessing.
_______Other

What elaborate plans did Rebekah and Jacob resort to in order to deceive Isaac? (Genesis 27:15–16)

______________________________________________

______________________________________________

As my mother used to say, "O, the tangled web we weave, when first we practice to deceive!"

Have you ever been caught in a web—either by your own choice or by someone else's actions? Think about that situation for a moment. Was there any justification for the lies? Did the ends justify the means? Were there consequences to be reaped?

Rebekah and Jacob still had time to turn away from the deception at this point, but they did not. One could almost hear their hearts pounding, for there is always great stress when sin is deliberate.

After Rebekah put the skins of the goats on Jacob's hands and on the back of his neck (remember, Esau was hairy all over like a garment), she gave Jacob the savory stew and freshly baked bread and sent him to Isaac.

When Isaac asked, "Who are you?" Jacob had to resort to lying (Genesis 27:19, 24). Who did he say he was? ______________________________________________

How do you picture Rebekah at this point?
_______ Standing by silently, coaching Jacob so as not to give away the deception
_______ anxiously scanning the horizon, watching for Esau to return from hunting in the fields.

Why? ______________________________________________

______________________________________________

I think if I were in Rebekah's sandals, I would be wringing my hands and motioning to Jacob to stop before it was too late. What if you were in Rebekah's place? What would you have done? ________

______________________________________________

______________________________________________

Even though Isaac was not thoroughly convinced that it was Esau (Genesis 27:24, 26–27), Isaac blessed Jacob, and Jacob went out. Jacob would be the head of the household, with all the legal rights and ramifications that accompany such a position.

The blessing included both a benediction and a prediction and was given in legal, irreversible form. Write the benediction as found in Genesis 27:28. ______________________________________________

______________________________________________

______________________________________________

Write the prediction from Genesis 27:29. ______________________________________________
____________________________________________________________________________
____________________________________________________________________________
____________________________________________________________________________

These same words echo Genesis 12:3. Who said these words, and to whom were they said? _______
____________________________________________________________________________

The plot thickened as Esau returned from hunting and prepared the game for his father. Esau took the savory game to his aging and nearly blind father and said, "Let my father arise, and eat of his son's game, that you may bless me." (Genesis 27:31)

Can you imagine the deafening silence at that moment? Isaac finally asked, "Who are you?" What did Esau reply? (Genesis 27:32) ______________________________________________

I find it interesting that Esau reminded his father that he was the firstborn, don't you? Do you think he was trying to justify to himself that even though he sold his birthright, he was still deserving of the blessing bestowed on the firstborn? Or do you think Esau was banking on the slim chance that Isaac did not know of the birthright issue?

How did Isaac respond to the words of Esau? (Genesis 27:33)______________________________
____________________________________________________________________________

Do you not think Rebekah's heart was wrenched within herself?

Esau cried out with an exceedingly great and bitter cry. What did Esau say to his father? (Genesis 27:34) ____________________________________________________________________

What did Isaac conclude? (Genesis 27:35)_____________________________________________

Read Genesis 27:36. Do you hear Esau's bitterness and anger towards Jacob? Esau wept loudly and pleaded for a blessing.

Isaac did indeed have a blessing for Esau, but it was not one that meant pleasantness. See Genesis 27:39–40: "Away from the fertility of the earth shall be your dwelling." The Edomites would occupy a territory less fertile than Canaan, live by the sword, and serve the people of Israel.

Can you imagine the extreme difficulty and sorrow Isaac suffered when he had to bestow such a blessing on his favorite son? Needless to say, Esau bore a grudge against Jacob—a grudge that festered into a plot to kill him.

How did Rebekah and her family come to such demise? Favoritism, self-gratification, jealousy, deceit, lies, anger, bitterness, quarreling, grudges, hurt, and a plan to murder! Families can run amuck when they veer off the right path, and how great a forest fire is set ablaze with a small spark. (James 3:5)

God had already chosen Jacob as the one He would bless through the covenant that He had made with Abraham and Isaac, since God knew of Esau's spiritual blindness and rebellious heart while he and Jacob were still struggling in Rebekah's womb. I often wonder how God would have brought about the blessing on Jacob rather than on Esau. One thing is certain—it would have been far better than the way the Isaacs handled it, wouldn't you agree?

## Discussion Question

Discuss ways people and families spiral out of control against the backdrop of Psalm 79:9.

## Personal Application Question

Do you ever feel that your sins may be too grievous for forgiveness? Read Isaiah 43:25 and respond.

Take a few minutes to write a prayer based on Psalm 103:12 and Ephesians 1:7.

Tomorrow we will see Rebekah, who upon meeting Isaac for the first time, behaved very becomingly - taking her veil and covering herself as a token of humility, modesty, and subjection, take action once again. Will it be to her delight or her downfall?

## DAY FIVE

# DECEIT AND ITS CONSEQUENCES

They have taught their tongues to lie; they weary themselves with sinning.
—Jeremiah 9:5 (NIV)

Yesterday we left Rebekah hearing the chilling words of Esau that he breathed to himself. "The days of mourning for my father are near; then I will kill my brother Jacob!" (Genesis 27:41)

This was neither an idle threat nor words spoken in the passion of the moment. Esau breathed these words of fire like a dragon spews flames before devouring its prey. Esau consoled himself this way as he waited and plotted for the right time to murder his brother—his twin brother.

When Rebekah heard these words from Esau, she sent for Jacob and said to him, "Behold, your brother Esau is consoling himself concerning you, by planning to kill you." Where did Rebekah tell to Jacob to flee to? (Genesis 27:43–44) ________________________________________

Do you recall Laban—Rebekah's brother and Abraham's nephew who lived in Mesopotamia—from day two of this week's study? Tuck his name in a side pocket of your memory for another glimpse into Rebekah's extended family and how it was steeped in the ugliness of deceit.

Read Genesis 27:45. Did you find anything preposterous in that verse? Look at Rebekah's words: "Until your brother's anger against you subsides, and he forgets what you did to him." Is it not human nature to blame someone else when we make a mess of things by our own choices? Adam blamed God for "the woman whom Thou gavest to be with me," (Gen. 3:12) and Eve blamed the serpent for deceiving her. Sarah blamed God for not giving her a son and impatiently took matters into her own hands.

This reminds me of a time when I was a teenager. A couple of girlfriends and I decided we would try smoking. I took one of my dad's cigarettes, and because both of my parents worked, we decided we would learn how to smoke at my house the following day. We sat around the kitchen table and practiced smoking. However, we coughed, gagged, and sputtered so much that we gave up, smashing the cigarette with the lipstick filter into the ashtray on the kitchen table. We then left.

My mother came home from work, saw the ashtray with the snubbed-out cigarette, and set it off to the side until after supper, at which time she nonchalantly set the ashtray in the center of the table and asked, "Whose is this?"

I immediately broke out into a sweat but answered, "Rob's." My brother shot milk out of his nose; he was flabbergasted that I would blame him for something that was obviously my doing. I did not have to plan what I was going to say. I just blurted it out. Maybe the same holds true for those we have read about so far. It seems like a natural thing to do, does it not? Can you think of a time where something similar happened with you? If so, write down one incident. ____________________

________________________________________

________________________________________

________________________________________

________________________________________

________________________________________

Blaming and deceiving are merely different forms of lying. What does God say about lying (or blaming or deceiving) in His Word? "Do not steal. Do not lie. Do not deceive one another" (Leviticus 19:11, NIV). "Friend deceives friend, and no one speaks the truth. They have taught their tongues to lie; they weary themselves with sinning" (Jeremiah 9:5, NIV).

Write Colossians 3:9. ____________________________________

________________________________________

God is serious about what He says to us in His Word. We ought to listen and be careful to obey His every word.

Rebekah went on to say, "Why should I be bereaved of you both in one day?" (Genesis 27:45) This was getting out of hand, and we can hear the fear in Rebekah's voice, since she knew that if Esau should kill Jacob, then the nearest elder relative would be obliged to avenge the murder and kill Esau. In that way, Rebekah would lose both sons.

Rebekah saw that the only way to save Jacob from death; Esau from committing his murder, was to deceive Isaac one more time. This time, she had to get Isaac to agree to send Jacob away. Look at her words in Genesis 27:46. "I'm disgusted with living because of these Hittite women. If Jacob takes a wife from among the women of this land, from Hittite women like these, my life will not be worth living" (NIV). Isaac took it from there.

Isaac called Jacob and charged him not to take a wife from the women of Canaan, but to "go to the house of Bethuel, your mother's father and take a wife for yourself from the daughters of Laban your mother's brother" (Genesis 28:1–2).

Isaac blessed Jacob with the words found in Genesis 28:3–4. "May God almighty bless you and make you fruitful and multiply you that you may become a company of peoples. May He also give you the blessing of Abraham to you and to your descendants with you; that you may possess the land of your sojournings, which God gave to Abraham."

Isaac sent Jacob away, and Rebekah *never* saw her cherished son again. Imagine Rebekah watching her son walk toward the horizon, not knowing that this would be the last time she would ever see him. Picture her with tears streaming down her face, hands clasped tightly over her heart, wishing with all her strength that Jacob did not have to be the one leaving but deceiving herself with the false comfort that Jacob would soon be returning.

Esau's predictable rebellion was flagrantly displayed once again. Read Genesis 28:8–9. When the Scriptures say that Esau went to Ishmael, they refer to Ishmael's family, since Ishmael himself had died fourteen years earlier. Remember, Ishmael was Isaac's half-brother—the son of Abraham and Sarah's maidservant, Hagar. Remember, too, that it was said that there would always be strife between the two peoples. Note that Esau did not put away his heathen wives when he married into Ishmael's family. Can you imagine the heartache this action of Esau must have caused Isaac and Rebekah?

Since Rebekah made herself vulnerable to us, we need only to glance in the nearest mirror and be reminded that *but for the grace of God, there go I.* In next week's lesson, we will trek with Jacob as he leads us to the next woman we will meet and spend time with.

## Discussion Question

Discuss the danger that is implied in the saying "The ends do not justify the means."

## PERSONAL APPLICATION QUESTION

Have you ever made a decision, either intentionally or unintentionally, that put someone else in harm's way? Has anyone ever made a decision, intentionally or unintentionally, that perhaps put you in harm's way? Without mentioning names, write of the situation and its results.

Take a few minutes to write a prayer, asking God for wisdom when making a decision.

# Week Four
# The Betrayal

Day One
**Jacob's Journey**

Day Two
**Jacob Meets Rachel**

Day Three
**Deception and Betrayal**

Day Four
**Facing the Past**

Day Five
**A Changed Heart**

## Day One

# Jacob's Journey

I am with you, and will keep you wherever you go.
—Genesis 28:15

Sarah's blessing to her unseen daughter-in-law, Rebekah, may have sounded something like this: "May you learn to wait upon the Lord in silence, and may your journey end in peace even as my journey ends in peace. The Lord God is faithful to His Word. Therefore, may you see the blessing given to Abraham and Isaac for descendants too numerous to count."

Sarah's last concern was for her beloved son, Isaac, and Rebekah's final regard was for her cherished son, Jacob. However, neither woman lived to see the fulfillment of God's covenant made to Abraham and to Isaac to bless them with descendants as many as the stars in the heavens.

This reminds me of my grandmother. As a very young girl, I spent precious hours with her while she stayed with my family for a short time prior to her death. I remember snuggling next to her, and in the dark quiet of night, she taught me to recite the twenty-third Psalm. I knew she prayed for me, too; I could hear her soft whispers in the stillness. Perhaps my grandmother prayed John 1:12: "Bountiful Father, draw my loved one to Jesus that she may receive Him; that she may believe in His name; that she would be given the right to become a child of You, O living God."[1]

Grandma must have sensed her time on earth was quickly drawing to a close, because she asked my mother to promise to send my older brother and me to a parochial grade school. My mother was faithful to her promise, and for all of my elementary school years, I learned *about* God and even memorized vast numbers of Bible verses.

I had head knowledge, but I did not have heart living until I was thirty years old. My grandmother prayed faithfully for me, but she never lived to see her prayers answered. How do you respond to prayers that seem to go unanswered? Could you trust God to work all things out for good—whether you see the results or not? ______________________________
Why or why not? ______________________________

______________________________

______________________________

Let's rejoin Jacob from last week's lesson as he travels to his mother's relatives in Mesopotamia. Remember that Jacob fled under Esau's threats to kill him because of his deception regarding the birthright. Jacob did not have time to gather belongings or servants but left with only his staff and the clothes on his back.

We come alongside Jacob as he heads toward Haran. The sun had set, and seeing that no one left the light on for him, he took one of the stones of the place and used it for a pillow.

Jacob had a dream while sleeping under the stars. He dreamed of a ladder or stairway set on earth with its top reaching to heaven, and angels were ascending and descending on it.
Above the ladder stood the Lord! The Lord identified Himself as the God of Abraham and Isaac and confirmed to Jacob the covenant. See Genesis 28:13–15. What did the Lord say He would give to Jacob? ______________________________
To what did the Lord compare the number of his descendants? ______________________________

______________________________

What additional promise did the Lord make to Jacob that He did not say to Abraham or Isaac? ___

______________________________

The Lord said, "And in you and in your descendants shall all the families of the earth be blessed." Read what the Lord spoke to Abraham in Genesis 22:18.

Read what Peter said in Acts 3:13, 25. According to Galatians 3:29, who are Abraham's offspring—heirs according to the promise? ______________________________

Do you see why God said the descendants of Abraham, Isaac, and Jacob would be as the stars of the heavens, the sand of the seashore, and the dust of the earth?

What was Jacob's reaction, and what did he say when he awoke from his sleep according to Genesis 28:16–17?______________________________

______________________________

What did Jacob do with the stone he used for a pillow? (Genesis 29:18) ____________________

______________________________________________________________________

The pouring on of the oil consecrated the altar. Jacob named that place Bethel, which means house of God. Do you think it is important to have a physical place to worship? Why or why not?______

______________________________________________________________________

______________________________________________________________________

Read Hebrews 10:24–25. Our place of worship in a corporate setting is the local church we attend. You will see the significance of Jacob's place of worship at Bethel later in our study.

Then Jacob made a vow. What words of God did Jacob repeat as stipulations that he would make God his God? See Genesis 28:20–21.

1. ____________________________________________________________
2. ____________________________________________________________
3. ____________________________________________________________
4. ____________________________________________________________

From whom do you think Jacob wanted safety when returning to his father's house?___________
What did Jacob say he would do with all that God would give to him? (Genesis 28:22) _________

______________________________________________________________________

Giving a tenth, or a tithe, was common among Semitic peoples and was an act that acknowledged the superiority of the one to whom it was paid.

God did indeed keep Jacob safe on his journey, providing food to eat and clothes to wear. For a peek into whether or not Jacob returned to his father's house, read Genesis 35:27. But that would be years down the road.

## Discussion Question

Describe what a beautiful person looks like to you.

## Personal Application Question

Have you ever had a dream in which it seemed that the Lord was speaking to you? If so, describe the experience.

Take a few minutes to write a prayer based on Luke 18:1, asking God to help you to persevere in prayer even if you do not see any results.

[1]Kroon, Rita. *Praying the Scriptures* (Denver, Colorado: Outskirts Press, 2011), 15–16.

## Day Two

# Jacob Meets Rachel

Leah's eyes were weak, but Rachel was beautiful of form and face.
—Genesis 29:17

As we begin our study, we will see that this is the day that was Jacob's most fortunate day! Let's join him as he continues his journey. He came to the land of the sons of the east. These people not only included the Midianites and the Amalekites, but also other nomads from the Syrian Desert region as well.

When Jacob looked up, he spotted a well in the field with three flocks of sheep lying beside it, for from that well, the shepherds watered the flocks. The stone on the mouth of the well was very large. When all the flocks were gathered there, they would then roll the stone from the mouth of the well, water the sheep, and put the stone back in its place on the mouth of the well.

Genesis 29:4–8 records Jacob's conversation with the shepherds. Jacob asked, "My brothers, where are you from?" They answered, "We are from Haran." Jacob asked, "Do you know Laban?" They replied, "We know him." Jacob asked, "Is it well with him?" They answered, "It is well, and behold—Rachel, his daughter, is coming with the sheep."

Listen with me as Jacob displayed his not-so-subtle cunning as he tried to get the men to leave before Rachel arrived. Jacob said, "Behold, it is still high day; it is not time for the livestock to be gathered. Water the sheep, and go pasture them." But the men said, "We cannot until all the flocks are gathered, and they roll the stone front the mouth of the well; *then* we water the sheep." Does his duplicity surprise you? Fill in the blanks from Isaiah 64:4: "For from of old they have not heard nor perceived by ear, neither has the eye seen a God besides Thee, who ____________ in behalf of the one who ________________ for Him."

While they were still speaking, Rachel came with her father's sheep. Jacob wasted no time swinging into action to try to impress Rachel. He went up to the well, singlehandedly rolled the stone from the mouth of the well, and watered her flock! Assuredly, Jacob noticed that Rachel was beautiful of form and face and had sparkling eyes.

Jacob kissed Rachel in greeting, and *then* he told her that he was a relative of her father's—that he was Rebekah's son. What did Rachel do? (Genesis 29:12) ______________________________

____________________________________________________________

Not long thereafter, as Jacob tended her sheep, Laban came running. Laban embraced Jacob and brought him back to his house to live. Jacob settled in, and after a month of working, Laban said to Jacob that just because he was a relative did not mean that he had to work for free. "Tell me, what shall your wages be?" Laban asked. (Genesis 29:15) When Laban said these words, he actually reduced Jacob to the status of a servant. Do you think Jacob met his match in Laban? We'll see.

By this time, of course, Jacob had met Leah, the older sister, but his heart belonged to Rachel. Since Jacob did not have enough wages to pay the customary price for a bride, Jacob said, "I will serve you seven years for your younger daughter, Rachel." (Genesis 29:18) Laban agreed. Can you imagine planning your wedding for seven years?

It is hard to fathom that the seven years went by quickly, for "they seemed like a few days because of his love for her" (Genesis 29:20).

Tell about a time when you waited with great anticipation for an event. Did the time seem to drag or go by quickly? ____________________________________________

____________________________________________________________

____________________________________________________________

____________________________________________________________

Mankind is governed by time. We have jobs, meet for lunch, go to doctor's appointments, gather for meetings, plan weddings, get children ready for school, and attend church and a host of other commitments, but I think Solomon said it best in Ecclesiastes 3:1–2 as he pondered the sovereign design of God and concluded that all the events of life are divinely appointed. "There is an appointed time for everything. And there is a time for every event under heaven. A time to give birth and a time to die." (Ecclesiastes 3:1) And there is a time for everything in between.

God has a timetable as well. Although God is not hindered or encumbered by time, His timing is crucial to His purpose! His purpose, according to Jeremiah 23:5, is that the Lord will raise up a righteous branch who will reign as ________________________, act as ______, and do justice and righteousness in the land. The English Standard Version says, "The LORD will raise up a righteous Branch and he shall reign as king and deal wisely and shall execute justice and righteousness in the land." The New International Version says, "The LORD will raise up a righteous Branch who will reign wisely and do what is just and right in the land." At the appointed time, God will raise up a righteous branch.

Let's not overlook God's timing as we take a look at the word B*ranch* of the Lord. I.e., Messiah; cf. Jeremiah 23:5; 33:15; Zechariah 3:8; 6:12, where the same term is found. The word *branch* is also used in this manner in Isaiah 4:2: "In that day the Branch of the Lord will be beautiful and glorious," in Jeremiah 33:15: "In those days and at that time I will cause a righteous Branch of David to spring forth," in Zechariah 3:8: "I am going to bring My servant the Branch," and in Zechariah 6:12: "Behold, a man whose name is Branch." This branch will reign as king. When is the time that God will raise up a righteous branch to reign as king? In that day, in those days, at that time—in other words, in God's exact, sovereign, pre-ordained time.

Who but Jesus is this righteous branch of the Davidic line of kings that will reign as King of kings and Lord of lords? According to Matthew 1:1–16, the genealogy of Jesus is traced from Abraham through 2,165 years to Joseph, Jesus' legal (though not natural) father, and it establishes His claim and right as king of the throne of David. Luke 3:23–38 apparently traces Jesus' genealogy through His mother, Mary, starting with Joseph and tracing back all the way to Adam. (Joseph was Jacob's son [not the Jacob of today's study] by birth and Eli's son by marriage.) Read Revelation 17:14, 19:16. What is the name written on Jesus' robe and on His thigh?___________ of __________ and ____ of ________________. Jesus, Son of God and Son of Man, is the King of kings and Lord of lords.

Jesus is king, but He also will simultaneously hold another office. For this reason, He had to be made like His brothers in every way in order that He might become a merciful and faithful high priest in service to God and that He might make atonement for the sins of the people (Hebrews 2:17). "Therefore, since we have a great high priest who has gone through the heavens, Jesus the Son of God, let us hold firmly to the faith we profess" (Hebrews 4:14, NIV). Also read Zechariah 6:13. What other office will Jesus hold?________________________________________________

God is not constrained by time to accomplish His purpose, but man is. However, during the seven years that Jacob worked for Laban for Rachel's hand in marriage, it must have *seemed* to Jacob as though he was not bound by time at all. He was willing to go through just about anything for the reward that awaited him!

How about you? Can you recall a time when you endured a particularly difficult hardship for the joy that awaited you? ________________________________________________

________________________________________________

"Let us fix our eyes on Jesus, the author and perfecter of our faith, who for the joy set before him endured the cross, scorning its shame, and sat down at the right hand of the throne of God" (Hebrews 12:2, NIV). See also Hebrews 7:21–22, 24, 26–27.

## Discussion Question

What was the joy Jesus anticipated while suffering on the cross? See Hebrews 2:10. Can you imagine the uncontainable joy when Jesus presents His bride, the church, to the Father?

## Personal Application Question

When are you most prone to ask, "Are we there yet?"

Take a few minutes to write a prayer asking God for patience based on James 5:7–8.

## Day Three

# Deception and Betrayal

What is this you have done to me?
—Genesis 29:25

We have been invited to attend a wedding—a wedding seven years in the making. The long-anticipated day had finally arrived!

The sheep had been shorn. The dark fleece had been washed and dried in the sun; it had been combed and spun into yarn for the tent that Jacob and Rachel would have on their wedding night. The flax had been harvested and made into fine linen for her wedding dress. The women were preparing the food for the wedding feast, and the choicest wine was in place. Laban made the arrangements for the wedding night. All was ready.[1]

After Laban had gathered all the men in the place according to their custom, they feasted the day away. You and I wait with Rachel in the evening for her father to come to escort her to the wedding tent. Our own hearts soar in anticipation of their pure love that will be made complete. Think of a time when you nearly burst with anticipation, and briefly describe such a time. ______________

______________________________________________________________________

______________________________________________________________________

The seemingly long hours dragged for Rachel. Evening turned into night. Night turned to dawn, and with the dawn came a nightmare—a nightmare so horrendous and incomprehensible that her words were strangled in her screams of betrayal! It was Leah who emerged from the wedding tent! (Genesis 29:25)

Laban had deceived Jacob. Instead of bringing his cherished Rachel to him, Laban brought Leah. We stand with Rachel in stunned silence as the deception and betrayal from her own father and her older sister nearly choked the life right out of her.

Being betrayed or deceived by a family member is like having salt dumped on deep wounds already laid bare—salt that does not bring healing but only immense pain, leaving untold scars hidden beneath the skin. A family should consist of people who love and care for one another, but as some of us may know from tragic experience, this is not always the case. I do not want to linger in an area that may be very sensitive to some, and I do not want to reopen hurtful memories at this time. We will tenderly acknowledge it for now and return to hopefully seek healing from the Lord later in today's study.

Let's turn our attention back to our account found in Genesis 29. Lies, betrayal, and deception seemed to linger in this family. We first witnessed this human default when Jacob deceived Esau out of his birthright. Then Jacob joined ranks with Rebekah when they lied and deceived Isaac into giving the blessing to Jacob. Thereupon, Rebekah had to deceive Isaac once again in order to have Isaac bless Jacob before sending him on his way and to prevent Esau from murdering her favorite son, Jacob.

Rebekah's brother, Laban, Rachel's father, took the reins of deception bridled with betrayal as he trampled his youngest daughter's dreams into muddy mire. Why? Why would Laban do such a thing? See Genesis 29:26. ______________________________________________

______________________________________________

Do you think Laban was: (Check all that seem appropriate.)
______ Trying to keep the tradition of marrying the oldest daughter first
______ Hoping to save face
______ Bringing happiness to his unbecoming daughter
______ Wanting to keep Rachel as shepherdess for his sheep
______ Other (explain) ______________________________________________

______________________________________________

How did Jacob respond? (Genesis 29:25)______________________________________________

______________________________________________

What is your first response toward a person who lies to you, deceives you, or worse, betrays you? __

______________________________________________

When a person betrays another, it is always activated by selfish motives. Let's examine the most flagrant betrayal of all time—Judas's betrayal of Jesus Christ. Let's look at Luke 22:48. Jesus said to him, "Judas, are you betraying the Son of Man with a kiss?" His motive was money. Luke 22:4–6 says: "And Judas went away and discussed with the chief priests and officers how he might betray Him to them. And they were glad, and agreed to give him money." Thirty pieces of silver, to be exact. But this was not the first time Judas dipped into the coffers to get money. John 12:4–6 gives us a very good description of the character of Judas. "But Judas Iscariot, one of His disciples, who was intending to betray Him, said, 'Why was this perfume not sold for three hundred denarii, and given to poor people?'" He said this not because he was concerned about the poor, but because he was a thief, and as he had the money box; he pilfered what was put into it.

Not long thereafter, Leah gave birth to a son, then another, and another, and finally her fourth son. What was Leah's vindictive motive for having sons born to her by Jacob? See Genesis 29:32–35. ___ It wasn't long before jealousy reared its head and snorted. Who became jealous of whom? (Genesis 30:1) ______________________________

One sister had Jacob's love; the other sister had his children.

What desperate tactic did Rachel implement that Sarah had also used with her husband, Abraham? (Genesis 30:3) ______________________________

After Rachel's maidservant bore Jacob two sons, how did Rachel feel? (Genesis 30:8) __________

______________________________

How did Leah retaliate? (Genesis 30:9) ______________________________

______________________________

After several years, Jacob had fathered six sons and one daughter with Leah, two sons by Rachel's maid, and two sons with Leah's maid. But Rachel was still barren.

Who intervened on Rachel's behalf? (Genesis 30:22) ______________________________

What was the result? ______________________________

What did Rachel name her son? (Genesis 30:24) ______________________________

______________________________

The unresolved tension between Jacob and his father-in-law, Laban, only escalated as time went on. How do *you* handle tension between family members? What if you were one of the ones involved in the conflict? Tension, like a faceless guest, sits at the table, pretending not to be there. This unwanted guest gets picked away at like one gnaws on a bone. Attention to tension causes dissension; conversations become trite. [1]Tension builds until it boils over in angry words that are harsh, accusing, cutting, and hurtful; [2]silence becomes deafening; [3]or tension is diffused through humble words of apology with a sincere desire for peace. Underline one of the three statements above that best describes how tension is usually handled in your family.

Jacob had become more prosperous than Laban, which only added to Laban's open hostility toward Jacob. Even Laban's sons threw accusations into the boiling pot. Read Genesis 31:1.

Who intervened? (Genesis 31:3) ____________ What did He say to Jacob? ________________

______________________________________________________________________

Who proves faithful regardless of man's actions? ____________________________________

When Jacob revealed his plan to return to his homeland, Rachel and Leah responded in agreement. Both sisters said that that their father "had sold them out and had entirely consumed the purchase price he had received on their behalf." They agreed to do whatever Jacob decided (Genesis 31:15–16).

Jacob gathered together Rachel and Leah, their maidservants, his children, and his flocks and herds and fled. Read Genesis 31:20. What did Jacob do to Laban? ___________________________

______________________________________________________________________

How? _________________________________________________________________
What did Rachel do? (Genesis 31:19) ________________________________________
Why do you think she did this? ____________________________________________

Did Jacob know Rachel did this? (Genesis 31:32) _____________________________

When Laban was told that Jacob had fled with all his belongings, his herds, his flocks, and Rachel and Leah, what did Laban do? (Genesis 31:22–23) _____________________________

______________________________________________________________________

Laban overtook Jacob and had a heated argument with accusations flying from both sides. See Genesis 31:25–42.

Why did Laban not find the idols that Rachel stole? (Genesis 31:34) __________________

______________________________________________________________________

What is the reason Rachel gave for not being able to stand in Laban's presence? (Genesis 31:35)____

______________________________________________________________________

But did Rachel have reason for not standing in her father's presence? We will see in tomorrow's lesson.

In the end, Jacob and Laban made a mutual, non-aggressive pact, calling God to be their witness. Even so, suspicion one for the other permeated their entire dialogue. Laban would return to his home, and Jacob would continue to his homeland with all his possessions. What was the total number of years Jacob worked for Laban? (Genesis 31:41) ________________________________

## Discussion Question

If *we* are the one in pain—whether physical, emotional, psychological, or spiritual—how can we seek help *from* others? Based on 2 Corinthians 1:3–5, how can we offer comfort *to others* who may be in a time of pain, whether physical, emotional, psychological, or spiritual?

## Personal Application Question

Is there a time in your life where you have been severely bruised and nearly crushed because of betrayal or jealously? Know that the Lord is tender toward you and the pain that you carry. He gives comfort in His Word through other believers who have suffered in similar circumstances and through Christian counselors who can lead you to restoration. Jesus loves you and will never forsake you. "The LORD himself goes before you and will be with you; he will never leave you nor forsake you. Do not be afraid; do not be discouraged" (Deuteronomy 31:8).

Take a few minutes to write a prayer, asking God to lead you to experience His tenderness, healing, strength, and courage.

[1]Kroon, Rita. *Letters from the Past* (Denver, Colorado: Outskirts Press, 2011), 42.

Day Four

# Facing the Past

Esau is coming to meet you and for hundred men are with him.
—Genesis 32:6

As we continue our journey with Rachel, her husband Jacob, her sister Leah, eleven children, their maidservants, other servants, and all the livestock, we sense uneasiness in the air. Rachel has bid goodbye to her father with many issues left unsettled, and certainly the apprehension of meeting Esau, Jacob's hostile twin brother, must have welled up within her soul as well. She naturally had concern for her one son, Joseph, her *pregnancy,* and traveling to a strange land. She was generally unsure of what the future held—whether real or unknown.

Perhaps you have unsettled issues that linger on the pages of your mind. If you had a spiritual ledger, would your "accounts payable" be checked as "paid in full," or is there unfinished business left to tend to—forgiveness, anger issues, jealousy, rebellion, unconfessed sin, or seeking forgiveness from another?

What causes you the most apprehension?

_______ Fear of the unknown
_______ Dread of a certainty
_______ Concern for what-ifs

Read Proverbs 31:25.

Who met Jacob and his company as they continued on their way? (Genesis 32:1)______________ We know nothing of these angels. How many were there? Why did they appear to Jacob? What did they say? We don't know where this took place, but we do know that Jacob named that place Mahanaim, which means double camps. See Genesis 32:2

One commentator says this about the angels: "They had invisibly attended him all along, but now they appeared to him, because he had greater dangers before him than those he had previously encountered."[1] We do know that whenever God sends his angels, He has a purpose for their encounters with man. Could it be possible that God intended to encourage Jacob for the pending encounter with Esau? Could it be that God was about to do a work in Jacob's heart? Or could it be that God is faithful to His covenant regardless of what man does or does not do? Is He not the God who promised that He would prosper Jacob with descendants too numerous to number, just as He promised to Abraham and to Isaac? Did He not say that His only begotten Son would come from the lineage of Abraham—from the line of the Jews? John 4:22 records Jesus' own words to the Samaritan woman: "You worship that which you do not know; we worship that which we know, for salvation is from the Jews."

What did Jacob do immediately after the encounter with the angels? (Genesis 32:3) ____________ __________________________ Notice how he manipulated what the servants were to say to Esau in Genesis 32:4: "Thus you shall say to my lord Esau: 'Thus says your servant Jacob.'" Remember when Jacob bartered a bowl of stew for Esau's birthright? And remember when Jacob deceived his father into giving him the blessing that rightfully belonged to Esau? Jacob remembered Esau's threat to kill him, and Jacob had ample reason to be frightened due to his prior lies and deceit. Jacob went on to list all his possessions. Does that not sound like a bribe—his possessions for Esau's leniency?

How many times do we try to bargain with God, promising that if He will deliver us from such-and-such, then we will do this and that? Dear one, this ought not to be. God does not bargain and cannot be bribed. There is nothing we can do to win God's favor, since all our righteousness is as filthy rags (Isaiah 64:6). Write Ephesians 2:8–9.

________________________________________________________________________________

________________________________________________________________________________

________________________________________________________________________________

________________________________________________________________________________

________________________________________________________________________________

Read Genesis 32:6. What did the messengers tell Jacob? ______________________________

________________________________________________________________________________

Terror gripped Jacob to his core! Rachel, no doubt, trembled with fear as well. Can you picture her gripping Joseph by his young hand and cradling her protruding belly with her other hand?

Jacob was operating in panic mode at this point. What did he do according to Genesis 32:7?

______________________________________________________________________

Why? (Genesis 32:8)______________________________________________________

______________________________________________________________________

After Jacob did all he could to ensure his family's safety, he prayed to God, saying, "O God of my father Abraham and God of my father Isaac, O LORD, who did say to me, 'Return to your country and to your relatives, and I will prosper you.' Deliver me, I pray from the hand of my brother for I fear him, lest he come and attack me and the mothers with the children" (Genesis 32:9, 11).

Jacob sent a most generous gift to Esau. What was Jacob hoping for? (Genesis 32:20) ___________ ________________________________________ Filled with uncertainty and fear, he sent Rachel and Leah, their two maids, and his eleven sons and one daughter across the ford of the Jabbok with whatever he had. Jacob was left alone, and it was night.

Tomorrow we will learn what happened with Jacob and the Lord, Jacob and Esau, and Rachel and her baby.

## Discussion Question

What if you've been wronged by someone, perhaps even more than once, and that person does not seek your forgiveness—is it possible to still forgive him or her? Explain.

## Personal Application Question

When faced with a seemingly impossible situation that causes you to be fearful or anxious, what do you do?

Read Psalm 139:23–24, and spend a few minutes in prayer, asking God to search your heart—to try your thoughts to see if there is any hurtful, offensive, or grievous way in you and to lead you in the way everlasting.

[1]Henry, Matthew. *Matthew Henry's Commentary on the Whole Bible* (New York: Fleming H. Revell, Co., n.d.)

Day Five

# A Changed Heart

Your name shall no longer be Jacob, but Israel.
—Genesis 32:28

As much as I'd like to stay huddled with Rachel, the other three women, and all their children, we are going to go back over the tributary of the Jordan to see how Jacob fared alone in the night.

We find Jacob wrestling with a man. Let's just sit quietly and watch. The two men wrestled for the entire night. Jacob agonized in prayer, weeping and imploring the man's favor. Suddenly, we hear a cry of pain, and we watch in silence. Jacob continued to wrestle with a dislocated hip! Genesis 32:25–28 describes the scene. Just before dawn, the man said, "Let me go, for the dawn is breaking." Jacob replied, "I will not let you go unless you bless me." So the man asked, "What is your name?" Jacob replied, "Jacob." Then the man said, "Your name shall no longer be Jacob, but ________________ ________________________; for you have striven with God and with men and have prevailed."

Why do you think the man dislocated Jacob's hip? Check all that may apply.

______ So Jacob would know the encounter was not a dream
______ So Jacob could not flee from Esau again
______ To change Jacob's belief that when all else failed, he should run
______ To bring Jacob to a place where he had to surrender
______ Other

Read Hosea 12:3–4. The man who wrestled Jacob is called an ________________________ We do not know for certain if indeed he was an angel or if perhaps he was the pre-incarnate Christ. I am certain, however, that Jacob's desperate prayers were for protection from Esau and that his life—along with the lives of his wives, their maids, and his children—would be spared, aren't you? But do you think Jacob also sought forgiveness and that by his asking for a blessing, he would be assured the protection and forgiveness that he so desperately needed? ________________________
Why or why not? ____________________________________________________________________

What name did Jacob give to the place where he wrestled with the man? (Genesis 32:30)__________

What was the reason? ________________________________________________________________

Jacob's name, which means "trickster," "heel catcher," or "supplanter" (to take the place of through plotting), was changed to *Israel,* which means "he fights or persists with God in prevailing prayer." (Genesis 32:28) Jacob was no longer the cheater, liar, and deceiver he once was but overcame his old, deceitful nature through the power of God.

"Therefore, if *anyone* is in Christ, he is a new creation; the old has gone, the new has come!" (2 Corinthians 5:17, NIV) One cannot encounter Jesus Christ and not be affected in some way or other, wouldn't you agree?

Have you ever persisted in prayer with God in a desperate situation? ________________________
Explain. __________________________________________________________________________

Have you personally (or has someone you know) ever experienced the power of God in a battle to overcome something that has held you (or the person you know) in bondage for any length of time?

Describe: ________________________________________________________________________

How do you (or someone you know) keep from going back into bondage? Write John 8:36.

___

___

___

After an exhausting and sleepless night, Jacob gathered Rachel, Leah, the maids, and his children with him. When he looked up, he saw Esau coming—and four hundred men with him! Jacob quickly divided the women and children, putting the maids and their children in front, then Leah and her children, and Rachel and Joseph last. But Jacob passed on ahead of them.

While Esau was a short distance away, Jacob bowed seven times, which was a sign of homage fit for a king. Jacob was taking no chances!

Read Genesis 33:4. How did Esau respond? ___

___

What did the two brothers do according to Genesis 33:4? They ___. Can you imagine the raw emotion after twenty years of separation and being reunited, forgiven, and restored?

Does this scene remind you of the Prodigal son? This young son left his father's house, taking his share of the inheritance and then squandered the money on loose living. Then after a famine and when the son was nearly starving to death, he returned home to his father. And how his father had waited for his son, watching the dusty road for any sign of him! One day, the father saw him and ran to meet him, embraced him, and kissed him (Luke 15:13–20).

Write Luke 15:10. ___

___

Genesis 33:6–7 portrays a very tender scene. "Then the maids came near with their children, and they bowed down. And Leah likewise came near with her children, and they bowed down; and afterward Joseph came near with Rachel, and they bowed down" (NASB). Do you picture tears of joy and relief streaming down Rachel's face? Can you feel her relief and her hope?

Esau had already seen the generous gift that Jacob had sent on ahead and asked Jacob, "What do you mean by all this company which I have met?" Jacob explained that he wanted to give Esau a gift, since he had received him favorably. What Jacob had first intended to be a gift of bribery became a gift given with sincere gratitude.

God told Jacob to take his family and go to Bethel, where God had confirmed the Abrahamic covenant to Jacob. Jacob was also to live there. Jacob was to take his household with him so that they could join in his devotion to God. Therefore, Jacob called for his entire household to prepare for the solemn occasion—to rid themselves of the foreign gods, purify themselves, and change their garments to rid themselves of any heathen practices.

Rachel took her earrings and the idols she had stolen from her father and gladly disposed of them with Jacob. Do you think Rachel ever told Jacob of the theft of her father's idols, or do you suppose Jacob met Rachel's eyes with sweet tenderness as she deposited the items onto the pile?

What did Jacob do with the foreign gods and the earrings? See Genesis 35:4.________________

______________________________________________________________________

______________________________________________________________________

As they traveled from Bethel toward Ephrath, Rachel started labor—a severe labor. (Ephrath is the ancient name of Bethlehem.) There was nothing anyone could do – not even her nurse. Her suffering was too great, and Rachel died in childbirth. However, she did live long enough to know that she gave birth to a son. Jacob named his twelfth son Benjamin. Jacob's sons became known as the twelve sons or the twelve tribes of Israel. The sons of Leah were Reuben, Simeon, Levi, Judah, Issachar, and Zebulun; the sons of Rachel were Joseph and Benjamin; the sons of Bilhah (Rachel's maid) were Dan and Naphtali; and the sons of Zilpah (Leah's maid) were Gad and Asher.

Levi became the priestly tribe; Moses, Aaron, and Miriam were from this tribe. Judah was the kingly tribe from which Jesus Christ descended.

Rachel was an example of the old adage that "love conquers all"—but not always without deep emotional scars along the way. Next week, we will start a new journey through time of over four hundred years and the distance from Bethel to the land of Goshen in Egypt in order to meet Miriam.

## Discussion Question

What do you think is the significance of the Lord changing Jacob's name to Israel?

## Personal Application Question

What descriptive name do you think the Lord would give to you and why?

Take a few minutes to write a prayer based on Mark 11:25.

# Week Five
# God's Dramatic Deliverance

Day One
**Young Heroine**

Day Two
**Deliverance Set in Motion**

Day Three
**On the Move**

Day Four
**Intercessory Prayer**

Day Five
**Restoration**

Day One

# Young Heroine

Shall I go and get one of the Hebrew women to nurse the baby for you?
—Exodus 2:7 (NIV)

We will divert our attention from the people of Israel in the land of Canaan to these same people in the land of Egypt, where we pick up our journey with a brief encounter with Joseph, Rachel's firstborn son. Let's skim the history of how and why the Israelites came to live in Egypt, since it is where we will meet Miriam, a woman of the priestly tribe of Levi who became instrumental in God's plan to rescue His people.

As you probably remember in the biblical account recorded in Genesis, Joseph was sold into slavery by his older brothers—Jacob's sons by Leah, her maidservant, and Rachel's maidservant. How did the older brothers feel toward Joseph? (Genesis 37:4, 11) ________________________________

________________________________________________________________

Jacob had sent seventeen-year-old Joseph to check on the welfare of his brothers as they tended their sheep. What was the brothers' first intention when Joseph was still a distance away? (Genesis 37:20)

________________________________________________________________

Who came to Joseph's rescue? (Genesis 37:22) ________________________________

They decided against murder, so they threw Joseph into a pit until they could come up with a plan to get rid of him. What did they do next? (Genesis 37:27) ________________________________

What does this one act tell you about the conscience and heart condition of the brothers toward Joseph? ________________________________________________________________

________________________________________________________________

Do you know or have you ever known someone who was *planning* to do a devious thing and to remain cold-hearted with no thought of the consequences? If so, briefly explain. ____________________

____________________________________________________________

____________________________________________________________

As the brothers ate their meal, a group of Ishmaelite traders passed by on their way to Egypt. (The Ishmaelites were descendants of Ishmael, Abraham's son with Hagar, who was Sarah's Egyptian maid.) Did the brothers succeed with their plan to sell Joseph into slavery? (Genesis 37:28) _______ For how much did they sell him? ____________________________________________

The redemption price of a mature slave was later set at thirty pieces of silver according to Exodus 21:32: "If the ox gores a male or female slave, the owner shall give his or her master thirty shekels of silver."

How noteworthy that Jesus, the Son of God, was sold for the price of a common slave. Matthew 26:15 records the transaction. Judas said, "What are you willing to give me to deliver Him (Jesus) up to you?" And they weighed out to him thirty pieces of silver.

Let's go back to our story of Joseph. He was a slave in Egypt for thirteen years before being promoted to the highest office under Pharaoh, because God was with him, and God gave Joseph the remarkable ability to interpret dreams with precise accuracy.

In fulfillment of the dreams given to Joseph, there came a seven-year period of plenty followed by a seven-year time of severe famine. But Joseph was directed by God to store an abundance of grain during the time of plenty for the famine years to follow.

Jacob, who was very old, sent his sons to Egypt to buy grain to sustain them during the famine. As it turned out after much testing, Joseph revealed himself to his brothers. What did he say? (Genesis 45:3)____________________________________________________________

Can you imagine the tension in that room? The brothers still felt guilty for selling Joseph into slavery more than twenty years prior, and Joseph stood before them, revealing who he was—their brother, the second most powerful man in all Egypt!

Guilt holds a person prisoner, and guilt does not go away with time; forgiveness sets one free! Have you ever had to forgive someone for wounding you, or have you had to seek forgiveness from one you may have wounded? ______ No matter which side of forgiveness we are on, forgiveness gives liberty and brings healing, wouldn't you agree? There cannot be forgiveness with our brother or sister if we do not first seek forgiveness from our heavenly Father. Read 1 John 1:9, and fill in the blanks. "If we ______________our sins, He is____________________ and ________________ to ________________us our sins and to cleanse us from all unrighteousness."

But forgiveness does not stop with seeking forgiveness only from God. If there is sin in our lives against another, we must confess it to the one we have wronged, seek forgiveness, and make any necessary restitution if possible. Read Matthew 5:23–24. What do these verses say we ought to do?_

________________________________________________________________________

________________________________________________________________________

Read Matthew 6:14–15. What do these verses mean to you? ______________________________

________________________________________________________________________

The Lord emphasizes the forgiving of one another. This is the forgiveness that affects fellowship within the family of God; not the forgiveness that leads to salvation.

Joseph forgave his brothers, saying, "Am I in God's place?" indicating that he should not withhold forgiveness. Joseph also gave clear testimony as to God's providential overruling in his life. See Genesis 45:5. According to Genesis 45:7, what reason did God have for sending Joseph to Egypt? ________

________________________________________________________________________

Joseph then sent for his father, Jacob, and his entire household, with all its flocks and herds, to come live near him in the land of Goshen, which was a fertile area in the eastern section of the Nile delta in Egypt. How many of Joseph's extended family members came to live in Egypt? (Genesis 46:27) _

________________________________________________________________________

________________________________________________________________________

Many years after Joseph and Pharaoh died, a new king arose over Egypt. The new Pharaoh wanted to make slaves of the sons of Israel for fear that they would become too many, join forces with Egypt's enemies, and overthrow Egypt. After three hundred years in captivity, the people of Israel were already a great number of people. The Israelites were organized into large labor gangs under cruel Egyptian taskmasters. Read Exodus 1:13–14. What did the Egyptian taskmasters do? __________________

________________________________________________________________________

________________________________________________________________________

________________________________________________________________________

To stop the multiplying of the Israelites, Pharaoh ordered all their male babies to be killed at birth. Now there was a man from the priestly tribe of Levi named Amram who married Jochebed. They had a beautiful baby boy, and Jochebed hid him for three months.

After three months, when she could no longer hide her son, she and her seven-year-old daughter, Miriam, made a waterproof basket, put the baby boy in it, and placed it among the reeds of the Nile River.

When Pharaoh's daughter came to the royal bathing area, she heard the cries of the baby and had her maidens retrieve the basket. Miriam hid in the nearby reeds and watched. When the basket was opened and they discovered it was a baby belonging to the Hebrews, Miriam stepped forward. After a brief dialogue regarding the baby, Miriam asked, "Shall I go and get one of the Hebrew women to nurse the baby for you?" (Exodus 2:7)

Pharaoh's daughter agreed, so Miriam ran to get her mother to come to take her brother back home and nurse him. At only seven years of age, what qualities did Miriam already exhibit? Check all you think apply.

_______ bravery
_______ leadership
_______ ingenuity
_______ compassion
_______ motivation
_______ other

The next time we meet with Miriam, she will be about eighty-seven years of age. Her brother, Moses, under the mighty power and direction of God, led the people of Israel out of Egypt after four hundred years of bondage. Miriam's other brother, Aaron, who was three years older than Moses and four years younger than Miriam, accompanied Moses to be his spokesperson. We will see how instrumental Miriam was in her later years during the exodus from Egypt, but I wanted you to get a glimpse of Miriam as a young girl first.

## Discussion Question

Do you know people who exhibited unusual qualities as a child that shaped their occupation or achievements in their adult lives? Explain.

## Personal Application Question

Do you ever feel that perhaps you have wasted years of training or education for something in which you are not currently being productive? Write of your experience.

Do not be discouraged. Nothing is ever wasted in God's economy. Even if you do not see the purpose for your training or your schooling play out in your current situation, God will use whatever He has provided for you to accomplish His purpose. Remember, too, that *our* purpose may not always be *His* purpose. Keep in mind as well that Moses spent eighty years in training, forty years in the Egyptian royal household, and forty years in the wilderness of Midian before he was called to carry out one of the greatest assignments given to man.

Take a few minutes to write a prayer, asking God that you would not be conformed to this world but be transformed by the renewal of your mind, that by testing, you may discern what the will of God is—what is good and acceptable and perfect (Romans 12:2).

Day Two

# Deliverance Set in Motion

Let My people go.
—Exodus 5:1; 6:11; 7:16; 8:1, 20; 9:1, 13; 10:2 (NIV)

God's mighty deliverance of His people from four hundred years of bondage in Egypt is just too magnificent not to linger here for a bit before moving on to spend personal time with Miriam. God's display of His power and might is too wonderful to miss!

How amazing that after being raised as a member of the royal household for forty years, Moses would still identify himself with the Hebrews! (Acts 7:23) Read Exodus 2:11-12. The Hebrews are called "his own people" in the New International Version and English Standard Version and "his brethren" in the New American Standard Bible and New King James Version. What did Moses see when he went to check on the Hebrew people? ______________________________

______________________________

What did Moses do?______________________________

______________________________

By this act, with whom did Moses cast his lot? ______________________________

When Moses struck down the Egyptian, that one act showed that he was not yet prepared to become their leader. What did Pharaoh do when he heard of the matter? (Exodus 2:15) ______________

______________________________

What did Moses do? ______________________________

The land of Midian was an area east of the Gulf of Aqaba or the Sinai Peninsula and was inhabited by the nomadic sons of Abraham with Keturah, his concubine, whom he may have married while Sarah was still living.

As Moses sat down by the well, seven sisters came to draw water and fill the troughs to water their father's flock. Wells must have been a popular place to meet prospective brides in those ancient days, wouldn't you agree? After all, Abraham's servant found Rebekah for Isaac at a well, Jacob met Rachel at a well, and now we see Moses at a well. Moses also had success at the well; he later married one of the sisters, Zipporah.

Moses settled down in Midian and raised two sons. He also pastured his father-in-law's sheep. How long did Moses dwell in Midian? See Acts 7:30. ______________________________

Moses spent his first forty years in Pharaoh's household and the next forty years in exile. Do you think in his wildest dreams that he ever considered going back to Egypt? Why or why not? ______

______________________________________________________________

What happened one day as Moses pastured the sheep? See Exodus 3:2 and Acts 7:30. __________

______________________________________________________________

What was so unusual about this particular bush? ______________________________

______________________________________________________________

I am reminded of the time when God got my attention in a most unusual way. Almost forty years ago, I was at a women's bowling banquet with my long-time girlfriend. She had mentioned several months prior that she had something very exciting to share with me, but we never seemed to have the time to sit down together and talk. But on this particular evening, we had the time. I had told my husband that I would be home around 11:00 p.m. Carol and I looked at our watches; both said 10:00, so we sat down to talk.

Carol told me how she had come to have a personal relationship with Jesus and about the joy not only in knowing where she was going to spend eternity, but also of the peace she found in a relationship with the Lord Jesus Christ. I listened intently to all she had to say. I was glad to hear her words of Scripture as she related its message to me in a way I had never before heard with such impact.

After what seemed a short while, we looked at our watches; it was nearly 11:00—time to go.

When I walked into my house a few minutes' drive from the bowling lanes, my kitchen clock said midnight! I looked at my watch—11:00. Just then, the phone rang. It was Carol. She asked me what time my kitchen clock said, and I told her midnight. Hers did, too. Then she asked me what time my watch said, and when I told her it was 11:00, she said with a tone of amazement, "So does mine!"

If both of our watches had said 11:00, we never would have taken the time to sit down together and talk, but they both said 10:00. How amazing!

That is how God got my attention! Two weeks later, I received Jesus as my Lord and Savior; I believed in His name, and I became a child of the living God (John 1:12).

What did God say that Moses should do? (Exodus 3:5, Acts 7:33) ______________________________

______________________________________________________________________

How did God identify Himself to Moses? (Exodus 3:6, Acts 7:32)______________________________

______________________________________________________________________

How did Moses respond? Check the answer that applies.

______ He was happy.
______ He shook with fear.
______ He built an altar.
______ He went merrily on his way.

What was God's intention? (Exodus 3:8, 10; Acts 7:34)______________________________

______________________________________________________________________

Why? (Exodus 3:7, 9; Acts 7:34) ______________________________________________

______________________________________________________________________

When God called Moses from the burning bush to go to Egypt to lead His people out of bondage, Moses came up with five excuses why he should not be the one to go, including the fact that he was not an eloquent speaker. He even pleaded that the Lord would send someone else. Then the anger of the Lord burned against Moses. "Is there not your brother Aaron the Levite? I know that he speaks fluently" (Exodus 4:14). That pretty much ended their discussion, wouldn't you say?

How about you? Have you ever experienced the Lord calling you to a specific task for which you felt inadequate, fearful, unwilling, or skeptical? What reasons did you give why you should, could, or would not do what you knew the Lord was clearly calling you to do? ______________________

______________________________________________________________________

What if you heard, "I AM WHO I AM has sent you?" (The inner meaning of Yahweh—"I Am the One who is"—emphasized God's dynamic and active self-existence. He is the everlasting Father. (See Isaiah 9:6.) How do you think you would respond? ______________________________

______________________________________________________________________

Let us go to Egypt, where Miriam and the rest of the Hebrews were struggling under the cruel taskmasters, and peek through the curtain of time to watch the incredible scene play out.

How did Aaron know that Moses was returning to Egypt? (Exodus 4:27) ____________________

________________________________________________________________________________

How did the people respond when they heard the words of the Lord given to Moses and related through Aaron? (Exodus 4:31) ______________________________________________

________________________________________________________________________________

What did Pharaoh say when Moses and Aaron approached him, asking him to let the people of Israel go? (Exodus 5:2) ________________________________________________________

________________________________________________________________________________

Not only did Pharaoh refuse to let the people go, but that same day, he also increased the workload of the Hebrews (Exodus 5:18). Because of the added harsh treatment, the people themselves did not listen to Moses and Aaron but blamed them for their increased workload. Moses was between a rock and a hard place, but with God, all things are possible.

How old was Moses when he first spoke to Pharaoh? (Exodus 7:7) ____________________
How old was Aaron? __________________________ That makes Miriam eighty-seven years old!

Pharaoh's heart was hardened, and refused to let the people go. So God sent plagues against Egypt. The first plague was turning the Nile River, streams, pools, and all their reservoirs of water into blood.

How long before the Lord sent the second plague? (Exodus 7:25) ______________________
Still, Pharaoh refused. Hence God sent a plague of frogs that swarmed up from the Nile and went into the Egyptians' houses and even into their bedrooms and on their beds. Pharaoh begged Moses and Aaron to plead with God to remove the frogs and said that he would release the people. God removed the frogs, but Pharaoh changed his mind.

So God sent the third plague—gnats like the dust of the earth. But Pharaoh's heart was still hardened. Thus God sent the fourth plague—flies and insects that devastated the land. But still, Pharaoh refused to let the people go.

Therefore, God sent the fifth plague—an infectious and fatal disease of all Egyptian livestock that affected their transportation, agriculture, and even worship, since cattle were sacred. Again, Pharaoh refused. Consequently, God sent the sixth plague—painful boils on man and beast. But Pharaoh's heart was hardened.

For this reason, God sent Moses and Aaron to Pharaoh with the words found in Exodus 9:16. Why did God allow Pharaoh to remain? ______________________________________________

______________________________________________

God sent the seventh plague—hail and flashes of fire that destroyed all the plant life and shattered every tree. Read Exodus 9:26. Remember when Joseph was the second-highest official in the land of Egypt and brought his father, brothers, and their families to Egypt? Where did he say for them to live? (Genesis 45:10)______________________________________________

______________________________ Goshen was not affected by the plagues against the Egyptians.

But Pharaoh defied the Lord. So God sent the eighth plague—locusts that covered the land and ate everything that had survived the hail. And still Pharaoh refused to let the Israelites go. As a result, God sent the ninth plague—three days of darkness that was so thick it could be felt. Yet Pharaoh's heart was hardened. Thus God sent the tenth and final plague—death of all the firstborn, even in Pharaoh's household.

At midnight, the angel of death struck down the firstborn of all the Egyptians so that there was no house where there was not someone dead. There was a great a cry and wailing from the Egyptians, but the angel of death *passed over* the houses of the Israelites, and not one firstborn was struck down, because the Israelites applied the blood of the sacrificial lamb over their doorposts, as God had commanded through Moses and Aaron.

According to John 1:29, who is the Lamb of God? ______________________________
What was His purpose? ______________________________________________
How did Jesus accomplish the Father's purpose according to Ephesians 2:13 and Colossians 1:20? _

______________________________________________

______________________________________________

What did He accomplish as stated in 2 Corinthians 5:19? ______________________________

______________________________________________

Where did this happen? Luke 23:33 says, "And when they had come to the place called Calvary, there they crucified Him, and the criminals, one on the right hand and the other on the left" (NKJV). Why? See 2 Corinthians 5:21. So that we might become ______________________________

______________________________________________

Those who are covered by the blood of the Lamb have their sins forgiven and are promised eternal life. Do you see the Bible's picture correlating the blood of the lamb, spread over the doorposts, saving those from death and Jesus' blood shed on the cross, saving us from God's wrath and eternal death?

Tomorrow we will be on the move, feeling the excitement in the air, tasting freedom, and walking alongside Miriam as we journey to the Promised Land.

## Discussion Question

Discuss your circumstances when God first got your attention and how you responded.

## Personal Application Question

Write of a time when you obeyed the Lord and received blessings as a result of your obedience.

Take a few minutes to write a prayer based on 2 Corinthians 9:13, asking that men will praise God for the obedience that accompanies your confession of the gospel of Christ.

## Day Three

# On the Move

The Lord heard your grumblings against Him.
—Exodus 16:7 (NIV)

Can you imagine 603,000 men, aside from women and children, escaping Egypt after four hundred years of captivity *led* by God Himself? The census at Sinai showed 603,000 males twenty years and older, and if that represented one fourth of the total population, the total number was likely around two million people on the move!

God led the people around by the way of the wilderness to the Red Sea to avoid the Philistines, "lest the Israelites change their minds when they see war, and they return to Egypt" (Exodus 13:17).

When Pharaoh realized that the people of Israel had fled, his heart was hardened, and he gave the order to pursue. Now the Lord led the Israelites by a pillar of cloud by day and a pillar of fire by night. But when the sons of Israel saw the Egyptian army marching after them and the Red sea before them, they cried out to the Lord. (Exodus 13:21, 14:10) Have you ever felt you were between a rock and a hard place? Explain.________________________________________

________________________________________________________

What did Moses say? (Exodus 14:14)____________________________________

The Lord told Moses to stretch out his hand over the sea. What did the Lord do? (Exodus 14:21)___

________________________________________________________

Why? (Exodus 14:22) ____________________________________________

When the Israelites reached the other side, what did the Lord say to Moses? (Exodus 14:26) ______

________________________________________________

What was the result? (Exodus 14:27) ________________________

Therefore, the Israelites sang a song of praise to the Lord for their deliverance. Read Exodus 15:20–21.
What is Miriam called? ________________________
What did she do? ________________________

________________________________________________

Once again, we see Miriam's leadership capabilities as she led the women in singing and dancing before the Lord in praise of His deliverance.

After three days in the wilderness, however, what did the people do? (Exodus 15:23–24)________

________________________________________________

After God led them to where there were twelve springs of water and seventy date palms, the people were refreshed.

On the fifteenth day of the second month after their departure from Egypt, what did the people grumble about? (Exodus 16:3)________________________
What did God provide for them? (Exodus 16:4) ________________________
What did the people call this "bread from heaven"? (Exodus 16:31) ________________

When the people reached Rephidim, what did the people complain about? (Exodus 17:1) ________
________________________ From where did the Lord provide water? (Exodus 17:6)

________________________________________________

Webster's Dictionary defines *grumble* as "to mutter or mumble in discontent; to complain in a surly or peevish manner."

One commentator writes,

> I think that this is something that we need to take into account when we're prone to complain about our lot in life. Who is it that has brought me here? Any complaining that I do is in reality complaining against God. For God is the One who has brought me to these circumstances. God is the One who has placed me here, unless I've been disobedient to Him. But my complaints are really against the Lord, and that's a very serious thing, to be complaining against God.[1]

Listen to what the Lord has to say about grumbling: The Lord spoke to Moses and Aaron, saying,

> "How long shall I bear with this evil congregation who are grumbling against Me? I have heard the complaints of the sons of Israel, which they are making against Me. Say to them, 'As I live,' says the Lord, 'just as you have spoken in My hearing, so I will surely do to you; your corpses shall fall in this wilderness, even all your numbered men, according to your complete number from twenty years old and upward who have grumbled against Me.'" (Numbers 14:26–29)

Let's flash forward to Isaiah 63:10 to see another instance when the Lord was grieved. "Yet they rebelled and grieved his Holy Spirit" (NIV). Psalm 78:40–41 says, "How often they rebelled against him in the desert and grieved him in the wasteland! Again and again they put God to the test; they vexed (pained, NASB) the Holy One of Israel" (NIV).

To understand what the Scriptures mean by "they put God to the test," let's turn to Numbers 14:22, where we read the words of the Lord: "Surely all the men who have seen My glory and My signs, which I performed in Egypt and in the wilderness, yet have put Me to the test these ten times and have not listened to My voice."

What was one of the gravest sins the people of Israel committed according to Numbers 14:27? ____

________________________________________

How does the Lord respond to grumbling and complaining of adversity? (Numbers 11:1) ________

________________________________________

The people were still pitying themselves rather than praising God for His power and deliverance from Egypt. "Then the sons of Israel spoke to Moses, saying, 'Behold, we perish, we are dying, we are all dying! Everyone who comes near, who comes near to the tabernacle of the LORD, must die. Are we to perish completely?'" (Numbers 17:12–13, NASB)

Followers of Christ who are called by God for a specific task will often endure hardships and obstacles. Read Acts 14:22. Peter was imprisoned (Acts 12:5); Paul was beaten on several occasions, shipwrecked, imprisoned, and in danger from rivers, robbers, his own countrymen, and the Gentiles. He suffered hunger, thirst, and spiritual pressures. See 2 Corinthians 11:23–27. John and Peter encountered persecution. See Acts 4:2–3.

What does Paul say in 2 Corinthians 4:17? ________________________________

________________________________________

When did the people arrive at Mt. Sinai? (Exodus 19:1–2) ________________________

The Lord called Moses from the mountain. Tell what the Lord required of the people as stated in Exodus 19:5: ________________________ and keep His ________________________

Describe the scene the people witnessed at Mt. Sinai. (Exodus 19:18–19)____________________

________________________________________________________________

After a time, Moses went up Mount Sinai to receive the Ten Commandments, which God Himself wrote on two tablets of stone. The people became impatient and restless when Moses did not return for forty days. What did they do? See Exodus 32:8. ________________________________

________________________________________________________________

________________________________________________________________

Who was instrumental in making the golden calf? (Exodus 32:2, 35) ____________ We can only surmise, but because of Miriam's influence on the women, she also may have been involved. Not only did the people worship the golden calf (idolatry) and offer sacrifices to it, but they also participated in drinking and immorality (Exodus 32:6).

What did the Lord do? (Exodus 32:35) ________________________________________

________________________________________________________________

Another time, the Lord struck down 23,000 who acted immorally (1 Corinthians 10:8). On another occasion, He struck down many with fiery serpents because of their grumbling and complaining (Numbers 21:5–6). Do you see how serious immorality and idolatry are in the Lord's eyes? Do you realize how serious it is to grumble and complain against the Lord for His provision for us?

Idolatry is anything or anyone who takes the rightful place of God. Colossians 3:5 says, "Put to death, therefore, whatever belongs to your earthly nature: sexual immorality, impurity, lust, evil desires, and greed, which is idolatry." 1Peter 4:3 says, "For you have spent enough time in the past doing what pagans choose to do—living in debauchery, lust, drunkenness, orgies, carousing and detestable idolatry."

Sketch a pie chart with five sections of various sizes. Label each section with activities you do in a typical week according to the time spent on each activity. Omit work done outside the home but do include such things as shopping, entertainment, prayer and Scripture reading, household tasks, and hobbies. Which slice takes up the most time? ____________________________________
Study your pie chart and ask yourself, "Could I have a golden calf?" If so, how has it usurped God's rightful place in your heart?

Let's fall into step with Miriam. As we travel with her, we notice that when the people first left Egypt, they had little sense of national identity and were used to obeying taskmasters; not following a man leading them to freedom. Moses' job was not an easy task. He needed all the support he could get, and the people needed constant reassurance that he was indeed chosen by God to take them to the

Promised Land. Imagine what would happen to Moses' confidence, as well as that of the people, if members of Moses' own family undermined his leadership by criticizing him in public! But that is exactly what happened!

Read Numbers 12:1. The verb *spoke* is feminine singular, indicating that Miriam led in this criticism. "Has the Lord indeed spoken only through Moses? Has He not spoken through us as well?" The Lord heard it!

At once the Lord said to Moses, Aaron, and Miriam, "Come out to the Tent of Meeting, all three of you." So the three of them came out (Numbers 12:4, NIV).

The Lord affirmed to Miriam and to Aaron (in earshot of Moses) that Moses was His servant—"very humble, more than any man who was on the face of the earth." The Lord asked Miriam and Aaron, "Why then were you not afraid to speak against My servant, against Moses?" (Numbers 12:8) And the anger of the Lord burned against them, and He departed. I can imagine Miriam and Aaron were speechless in their defense, can't you?

What happened immediately after the Lord's departure? See Numbers 12:10. ________________

________________________________________________

Miriam was shut outside the camp for seven days according to the laws concerning leprosy. Can you imagine the shame and humiliation Miriam must have felt, since the entire camp of people knew of her criticism of Moses?

Many of us may not recognize our bent to grumble and complain, commit idolatry, be jealous, and criticize, but unless we are perfect, the bent is there!

## Discussion Questions

1. What insight did you gain from the examples of grumbling and complaining that you can apply to your own responses to unpleasant situations? Since it is God who is at work in us, both to will and to work for His good pleasure, ought we not do all things without grumbling and complaining? (Philippians 4:13–14) Shouldn't we cultivate a joyful heart as good medicine for the soul? (Proverbs 17:22)

2. Discuss "valid insight given with a loving spirit" versus "being openly critical." In times when we find fault with someone, should we not remind ourselves that in the same way we judge others, we will be judged? (Matthew 7:2) And if we bite and devour one another, we will be devoured. (Galatians 5:15)

## Personal Application Question

Recall times you may have been critical of another person. What do you think may have been an underlying attitude that caused you to criticize? Would it not be better to put on a heart of compassion, kindness, humility, gentleness, and patience, bearing with one another and forgiving one another? (Colossians 3:12–13)

Take a few minutes to pray, asking God to "Show me your way, Lord, that I may know you and know what pleases you (Exodus 33:13). Open my eyes to your goodness, grace, and mercy so that I may give praise and thanksgiving rather than grumble and complain. Heighten my awareness of my *motives* in speaking against others, and show me how to offer constructive suggestions in love rather than negative criticism."

Tomorrow, we will witness a most amazing thing on Miriam's behalf! You won't want to miss it.

[1]Smith, Chuck, *Exodus 16-18* (Costa Mesa, CA: The Word For Today, 2000)

Day Four

# Intercessory Prayer

And Moses cried unto the LORD, saying, "Heal her now, O God, I beseech thee."
—Numbers 12:13 (KJV)

Yesterday, we left Miriam in isolation for seven days because of her leprosy, which she received for criticizing Moses, the servant of the Lord. Her underlying cause for criticizing her youngest brother was jealousy. Why? Numbers 12:2 gives us a clue. "Has the LORD indeed spoken only through Moses?" they asked. "Has He not spoken through *us* as well?" Notice Miriam included Aaron in this word-assault against Moses. In other words, "What about us?"

Were Miriam and Aaron venting against Moses only to each other? Could they have been speaking to the people stirring up dissension, trying to reestablish their own creditability, desiring more recognition, wanting God to speak with them as He did with Moses—face-to-face? Read Ephesians 4:29.

Moses had cried out to the Lord in Numbers 11:14, saying, "I alone am not able to carry all this people, because it is too burdensome for me." The Lord responded, and instead of choosing Miriam and Aaron to help Moses, whom did He say to choose? (Numbers 11:16) ____________________

________________________________________________________________________________

God, in His infinite wisdom, knew the task of assisting Moses was too great a burden for Miriam and Aaron to handle; seventy elders were needed to assist the overwrought prophet. Could it be that Miriam and Aaron did not see God's wisdom in this situation—that perhaps they felt they should have been officially appointed as capable assistants? Could the seed of jealousy have been planted here?

Soon Moses' private life became a source of contention. Why? Since Moses was a humble man and did not flaunt his leadership role, family, or relationship with the Lord, could it be that Miriam and Aaron picked up on the fact that Moses was seemingly happily married to a Cushite woman (probably Zipporah, whom he married after fleeing Egypt)? Soon Moses' private life snowballed into jealousy of Moses' status over the multitude of people—a position that nearly broke Moses except for the intervention of the Lord on his behalf.

Yet God is a jealous God, is He not? "Therefore thus says the Lord GOD: 'Now I will bring back the captives of Jacob, and have mercy on the whole house of Israel; and I will be jealous for My holy name'" (Ezekiel 39:25, NKJV).

The difference is that God is jealous *for* His holy name and His people; not wanting what is good for Himself but for the benefit of another. Human jealousy is of another's status; wanting something for *oneself*—having an intense interest in another's honor or prosperity.

What would be your response if your status or position were threatened? For example, what if your authority over disciplining your children was undermined or your position at work was threatened by a co-worker or your integrity was attacked by a jealous person? Briefly explain. ____________

______________________________________________________________________________

______________________________________________________________________________

______________________________________________________________________________

______________________________________________________________________________

______________________________________________________________________________

Have *you* ever been jealous of someone else's success? How did you react? ________________

______________________________________________________________________________

______________________________________________________________________________

______________________________________________________________________________

______________________________________________________________________________

Let's look at what happened after the Lord departed in anger toward Miriam and Aaron. Numbers 12:10 says, "As Aaron turned toward Miriam, behold, she was leprous." Can you imagine the horror on his face? Can you picture Miriam looking in total dismay at her rotting flesh on her hands and arms, feet, and legs? Even Moses must have gasped.

Hear the anguish in Aaron's words when he spoke to Moses as you read Numbers 12:11–12. And what did Moses do? He immediately cried out to the Lord, saying, "O God, heal her, I pray!" (Numbers 12:13)

With love and compassion, the two brothers came to Miriam's aid in desperate prayer on her behalf. Aaron confessed their sins and pleaded for forgiveness; Moses interceded for healing.

Miriam paid the consequences for her sins but was forgiven and eventually restored. The Lord said in Numbers 12:14, "Let her be shut up for seven days outside the camp, and afterward she may be received again." Leviticus 13:2–14 details the instructions for dealing with leprosy, which included isolation of the unclean person for seven days. The fact that leprosy was loathsome and had attached stigma and taboos strongly suggests that it may have served as an illustration of sin. Leviticus 14:1–57 also gives detailed and elaborate instructions for the cleansing of a leper if you care to read all the instructions.

As we plan to take leave of our long journey with Miriam, what did you find most appealing about her? ____________________________________________

____________________________________________

What characteristics did you find least acceptable? ____________________________

____________________________________________

What did you discover about Miriam that you see in yourself? ____________________

____________________________________________

____________________________________________

____________________________________________

With what part of her struggles do you most readily identify? ____________________

____________________________________________

____________________________________________

## Discussion Question

What insight did you gain regarding Aaron and Moses from their response to Miriam's leprosy? Isaiah 41:10 is a beautiful verse to use as an intercessory prayer. "Father in heaven, I pray that my friend/loved one would fear not nor be dismayed. I ask that you would strengthen her—that you would help her; that you would uphold her with your righteous right hand. Reveal yourself as her God—a very present help in the time of trouble."[1]

## Personal Application Question

If you were the one who was offended and something tragic happened to the person who wronged you as a direct result of his or her offending you, how would *you* react toward that person?

"Sovereign God, give me a heart to love my enemies; to do good and sin not. Put a generosity within me that I may lend without expectation of anything in return, for you have demonstrated your kindness to ungrateful and evil men. Therefore, I desire to learn love and kindness from you (Luke 6:35)."[2]

Take a few minutes to write a prayer based on Romans 15:1–2, asking God to inspire you to pray on behalf of another for his or her good even if that person has wronged you.

[1] Kroon, Rita. *Praying the Scriptures* (Denver, Colorado: Outskirts Press, 2011), 15.

[2] Kroon, Rita. *Praying the Scriptures* (Denver, Colorado: Outskirts Press, 2011), 51.

## Day Five

# Restoration

The Lord bless you, and keep you.
—Numbers 6:24

Could God's deliverance of believers from the bondage of sin be any less dramatic than His deliverance of the Israelites from their bondage of slavery in Egypt? Could His victory over death at Calvary be any less profound than His victory over the Egyptians at the Red Sea? Could God's vow to bring us to the Promised Land be any less sure now than His pledge to the Israelites to bring them to the Promised Land in 1400 BC? Could His provision for our redemption be any less essential than His provision for thousands of people in a wilderness for forty years? Could God's loving kindness toward us be any less a surety now than His loving kindness was for the people of Israel? Could His holiness be any less holy now than it was during the Exodus? Could God's purpose and plan be any more likely to be thwarted now than it was at the beginning of creation?

Jesus said in Matthew 5:18, "For truly, I say to you, until heaven and earth pass away, not an iota, not a dot, will pass from the Law until all is accomplished" (ESV). Consider these words of Isaiah: "Have you not known? Have you not heard? The LORD is the everlasting God, the Creator of the ends of the earth. He does not faint or grow weary; his understanding is unsearchable" (Isaiah 40:28, ESV). Listen to God's words in Isaiah 46:9–10: "Remember the former things of old; for I am God, and there is no other; I am God, and there is none like me, declaring the end from the beginning and from ancient times things not yet done, saying, 'My counsel shall stand, and I will accomplish all my purpose'" (ESV).

What, then, is God's purpose? Listen to the words of Peter found in Acts 2:23: "This Man (Jesus) was handed over to you by God's set purpose and foreknowledge; and you, with the help of wicked men, put him to death by nailing him to the cross." The New American Standard Bible says "predetermined plan," the English Standard Version uses "definite plan," and the New King James Version says "determined purpose." Colossians 1:20 declares the purpose of God: "And through Him (Jesus) to reconcile all things to Himself… To present us before Him holy and blameless and beyond reproach" (Colossians 1:22). Ephesians 5:27 says, "That He might sanctify her (the church) … that He might present to Himself the church in all her glory, having no spot or wrinkle or any such thing: but that she should be holy and blameless."

Why does God want to reconcile or restore us to Himself? Beloved, read the words of John in 1 John 4:8: "For God is love." Write John 3:16. ______________________________

______________________________

______________________________

It is God's nature to love, but since He is holy, He cannot be in the presence of sin—our sin, your sin, my sin, any sin. He loves us but cannot allow us in His presence with our sin, and since we cannot do away with our sin by ourselves, how does He remedy this situation? Through the blood of His (Jesus) cross—through Him (Colossians 1:20). Write 2 Corinthians 5:17. ______________

______________________________

______________________________

______________________________

According to the above verses, what is God's purpose? ______________________

______________________________

Why? ______________________________

How? ______________________________

Read Acts 10:43. What must we do to be saved? See John 1:12 and Acts 16:31. ____________

______________________________

What instruction did God give to the people of Israel through Moses found in Deuteronomy 6:5; 11:1, 13? ______________________________

______________________________

______________________________

What command does God give to us in 1 John 3:23? ______________________

______________________________

How are we to love one another? See John 13:34. ______________________

What causes God's wrath? See Deuteronomy 9:7, 11:16; Hebrews 3:19, 4:6. ________________
________________________________________________________________. Is it not all the sin of thought, word, and deed that causes God's wrath? We have already noted how grumbling and complaining displeased the Lord, but what about criticizing? Webster's Dictionary defines *criticism* as "to judge disapprovingly; to find fault." Scripture says "to speak against," (Numbers 12:8, NSAB) but the exact connotation is "criticize." When Miriam spoke words of criticism against Moses, what did God say to her? (Num. 12:8) ________________________________________
________________________________________________________________
________________________________________________________________

Because of their words of criticism against Moses, the Lord's anger burned against Miriam and Aaron.

How is God's wrath appeased? Second Chronicles 7:14 says, "If my people, who are called by my name, will humble themselves and pray and seek my face and turn from their wicked ways, then will I hear from heaven and will forgive their sin and will heal their land."

God made Him (Jesus) who had no sin to be sin for us so that in Him, we might become the righteousness of God (2 Corinthians 5:21, NIV). When Jesus took all our sins upon Himself, the full wrath of God was poured out on Jesus! The Father had to turn away from His beloved Son; He could not even look upon Jesus because of our sin. Hence, Jesus cried aloud, "My God, My God, Why have You forsaken Me?" (Mark 15:34) Do you hear His anguish? Do you feel His pain? Jesus satisfied the full wrath of God against all sin!

First John 4:9–10 says, "This is how God showed his love among us: He sent his one and only Son into the world that we might live through him. This is love: not that we loved God, but that he loved us and sent his Son as an atoning sacrifice for our sins (as the one who would turn aside His wrath, taking away our sin)" (NIV).

Read Romans 5:8–11.

Numbers 12:15 says, "Let her be shut up for seven days outside the camp, and afterward she may be received again." What do you think it means to be received again? Check the appropriate answers.

_______ She would be allowed to dance
_______ She would be reconciled
_______ She would be endured
_______ She would be restored
_______ She would be held in contempt

How about you and me? How are we reconciled to God? See John 1:12, Ephesians 2:8–9, and 2 Corinthians 5:20–21. ______________________________

______________________________

After more than eighty years living in Egypt and forty years in the wilderness, we say goodbye to Miriam at her death in the wilderness of Zin. Numbers 20:1 simply says, "Now Miriam died there and was buried there." It goes on to say, "And there was no water for the congregation; and they assembled against Moses and Aaron." There was no mention of mourners at her death—only that the congregation was grumbling again for lack of water.

## Discussion Question

Do you think the Old Testament reveals the wrath of God, or do you see His immeasurable patience and longsuffering? Why?

## Personal Application Question

How do you know you have been reconciled to God?

Take a few minutes to write a prayer based on John 10:27–30, asking God to assure you of your reconciliation with Him. If you have never been reconciled to God, perhaps you would like to ask God to reconcile you to Himself by confessing your sins to Him and asking Him to forgive you, believing that Jesus has paid the penalty for your sins and humbly receiving the gift of salvation that He offers through His shed blood on the cross.

# Week Six
# Era of the Judges

## Day One
### Background

## Day Two
### Deborah—Judge of God's People

## Day Three
### Deborah—Military Commander

## Day Four
### The Battle Belongs to the Lord

## Day Five
### Learning from Deborah

## Day One

# Background

I will never break My covenant with you.
—Judges 2:2

Though the Promised Land had been generally conquered and occupied by the people of Israel after their miraculous delivery from Egypt and their forty years in the wilderness, certain Canaanite strongholds still remained. The subduing of these Canaanite pockets, albeit unsuccessful, was left to individual Israelite tribes that were allotted particular parcels of land that housed the enemy. The enemy became an entrapment for the sons of Israel and a constant source of idol worship influence. Consequently, the Lord's anger was kindled against the Israelites. He would give them to the hands of their enemies, and they would be oppressed for years at a time.

Israel was commanded to utterly destroy the Canaanites when they took possession of the Promised Land. They were commanded:

> "You shall defeat them, then you shall utterly destroy them. You shall make no covenant with them and to show no favor to them. Furthermore, you shall not intermarry with them; you shall not give your daughters to their sons, nor shall you take their daughters for your sons. For they will turn your sons away from following Me to serve other gods; then the anger of the Lord will be kindled against you, and He will quickly destroy you … You shall tear down their altars, and smash their sacred pillars, and hew down their Asherim (associated with Baal worship; the Asherim were images of Asherah, the mother of 70 gods, including Baal). (Deuteronomy 7:2–5)

Why were they commanded to do this? See Deuteronomy 7:6. ______________________________

_____________________________________________________________________________

What does Deuteronomy 7:9 say about the Lord God? _________________________________

_____________________________________________________________________________

What happens to those who hate the Lord God? (Deuteronomy 7:10)______________________

_____________________________________________________________________________

What about those who keep His statues and commandments? (Deuteronomy 7:13)____________

_____________________________________________________________________________

It was during this turbulent time, when "every man did what was right in his own eyes" (Judges 17:6, 21:25) that the Lord raised up judges to rule over His people (Judges 2:16). These judges served as spiritual, military, and governmental leaders for the people but were often ignored or rejected (Judges 2:17). The judges God gave Israel are also called deliverers (Judges 3:9). This era of judges covers the period in Israel's history from about 1380 to 1050 BC. Historically, the book of Judges links the conquest of the Promised Land (Palestine) to the beginnings of the monarchy (kings).

God's faithfulness was not based on the obedience of His people; rather, the enjoyment of His blessings toward His people was conditioned on their obedience.

What attributes of the Lord God are displayed during the times when the people continually did what was evil in the sight of the Lord and the times He delivered them repeatedly from bondage? Check all that apply.

_______ Long-suffering
_______ Righteousness
_______ Justice
_______ Sovereignty
_______ Patience
_______ Faithfulness
_______ Mercy
_______ Graciousness
_______ All-knowing
_______ Love
_______ Anger
_______ Holiness

The command to love the Lord found in Deuteronomy 6:5 says, ____________________________

_____________________________________________________________________________

When Jesus was asked by one of the Pharisees, "Which is the great commandment in the Law," how did Jesus respond? (Matthew 22:37) __________________________________________________

_____________________________________________________________________________

According to Jesus' words in Matthew 22:39, what is the second great commandment? ________

________________________________________

What is dependent on these two commandments? (Matthew 22:40)________________

________________________________________

Isn't it amazing that if we just keep these two commandments, there would be no need for any other commandment? If we loved God first and loved others as He has loved us, we would serve God with all our hearts and souls, and we would esteem others above ourselves. There would be no idolatry, rebellion, pride, selfish ambition, or crime done to others. The good news is that this *will occur* during the future thousand-year earthly reign of Christ (millennium) in fulfillment of the Abrahamic and Davidic covenants of the Old Testament and the new covenant of the New Testament, which is the cross of Christ.

The New Testament literally means "the new covenant." The word *covenant* meant an arrangement made by one party that the other party involved could accept or reject but could not alter. The old covenant revealed the holiness of God in the righteous standard of the Law and promised a coming Redeemer; the new covenant shows the holiness of God in His righteous Son.

Do you recognize God's incomprehensible grace to those who live in the church age? Do you perceive God's immeasurable mercy to us? Remember, grace is getting what we don't deserve (kindness), and mercy is not getting what we do deserve (punishment).

Tomorrow, we will see God graciously provide leaders and judges for the Israelite nation, which was a loose confederacy at best.

## Discussion Questions

Who will reign during the millennium? (Revelation 3:21) ________________________

From where will Jesus reign? (Revelation 21:2, 10) ________________________

Who will reign with the King of kings? (Revelation 3:21, 1 John 5:5)________________

________________________________________

What will all believers see? (Revelation 22:4) ________________________

There will be fullness of life and continuous blessing! (Revelation 22:1–2) This kingdom will bring in peace, equity, justice, prosperity, and glory. Discuss your concept of this thousand-year earthly kingdom.

## Personal Application Question

What emotions are stirred within your heart as you know that you, as a believer, will reign with Christ, the Lord of lords and the King of kings, for a thousand years? (Revelation 20:6)

Take a few minutes to write a prayer of praise and worship based on Revelation 15:3–4.

## Day Two

# Deborah—Judge of God's People

Therefore, you are to be perfect, as your heavenly Father is perfect.
—Matthew 5:48

There were several judges who ruled over the people of Israel. Because of their evil in the sight of the Lord, what did the Lord do? (Judges 3:8) ________________________________________

________________________________________________________________________

For how long?________________________________ Othniel (Judges 3:7–11) was the first judge God called to deliver the sons of Israel from the king of Mesopotamia. How long did the land have rest under Othniel? (Judges 3:11)________________ History repeats itself; the sons of Israel again did evil in the sight of the Lord. This time, it was the king of Moab who oppressed the Israelites. For how long did he oppress them? (Judges 3:14) ______________ Who did God raise up to deliver the people? (Judges 3:15) ________________________What unique characteristic is noted about Ehud? _____________ How long did the land go undisturbed? (Judges 3:30) ______________

The next judge to save Israel was Shamgar, who defeated the Philistines, although it is not clear when he ruled or for how long. See Judges 3:31. Again, the people of Israel did evil in the sight of the Lord. This time, He sold them into the hand of Jabin, king of Canaan. His commander, Sisera, was skilled and had disciplined soldiers who were armed to the hilt with weapons and iron-trimmed chariots. At just the mention of Sisera's name, terror spread like black storm clouds over the land. It was reported that the mighty Canaanite army possessed nine hundred chariots that were ready for battle.[1] Israel was severely oppressed for twenty years. This is the time and the place in history where we meet Deborah, the fourth judge over Israel.

What two things are mentioned about Deborah in Judges 4:4?_________________________and _____________________ As a prophetess, Deborah did not foretell future events; rather, she heard messages from God and simply and obediently repeated the words of God to the people. These were usually words of warning to separate themselves from the wicked people around them, especially in the hill country of Ephraim; sometimes they were words of military strategy. Deborah recognized that she had no authority of her own but only that which had been given to her by God.[2]

Where did Deborah hold her office while attending to civil matters? (Judges 4:5)

_____________________________________________________________

The palm of Deborah was located between Ramah and Bethel in the hill country of Ephraim. Whenever she sat under the palm tree, people came to her with their matters of dispute that could not be resolved in the lower courts. She listened intently to the disputes, whether sacred or civil, and sought God's wisdom before pronouncing her judgment.

Deborah herself had to be judged as a woman of holy integrity and knowledge of the laws of God in order to be found worthy and qualified for judging the people according to the laws of God. She was continually under scrutiny and was mindful of the great responsibility placed upon her. She would have been under indictment herself except for the hand of God upon her.

God had given her great authority rather than power over His people, which prepared her to defend and rescue God's people from their enemies. She did not think more highly of herself than she ought, for she knew her appointment was from God, and she had to give an account to Him as Lord. The responsibility of the call to be judge over Israel far outweighed any pomp she might have considered a thing to be grasped.[3]

On a much grander scale, Jesus, Son of God, although He existed in the form of God, did not regard equality with God a thing to be grasped (Philippians 2:6, NASB). In other words, neither Deborah nor Jesus exploited their position for their own personal gain.

Tomorrow, we will see Deborah in a role occupied only by men to this point. We will watch Deborah in action as military leader of the people of Israel.

## Discussion Question

What does it mean to be true to yourself at all times and in all situations?

## Personal Application Question

Would you ever want to be in a position of public authority? Why or why not?

Take a few minutes to write a prayer, asking God to reveal an area of your life about which you would be embarrassed or ashamed if it came under scrutiny.

[1] Kroon, Rita. *Letters from the Past* (Denver, Colorado: Outskirts Press, 2011), 108.

[2] Kroon, Rita. *Letters from the Past,* (Denver, Colorado: Outskirts Press, 2011), 107.

[3] Kroon, Rita. *Letters from the Past,* (Denver, Colorado: Outskirts Press, 2011), 107–108.

## Day Three

# Deborah—Military Commander

Behold, the Lord, the God of Israel, has commanded.
—Judges 4:6

Today, we will have to put our marching boots on if we are going to spend time with Deborah. According to Judges 4:6, what was the name of her right-hand military man? ____________

One day, the Lord spoke to Deborah concerning a military matter. According to Judges 4:6–7, Deborah summoned Barak and said, "Behold, the Lord, the God of Israel, has commanded, 'Go and march to Mount Tabor, and take with you ten thousand men from the sons of Naphtali and from the sons of Zebulun. And I will draw out to you Sisera with his chariots and his many troops to the river Kishon and I will give him into your hand.'" Notice how Deborah prefaced her orders to Barak: "the Lord, the God of Israel, has commanded." Deborah received her marching orders from the Commander-in-Chief.

Even though Barak *heard* the words of the Lord, "I will give him into your hands," he *knew* that the enemy had nine hundred iron chariots and all the people to go with them in addition to all the foot soldiers! (Judges 4:3, 13)

How many men was Barak supposed to deploy from the two tribes of Naphtali and Zebulun? ____ ________________________________ What words of hesitation did Barak say? (Judges 4:8) ________________________________________________________________

Remember, from Barak's perspective, Israel had only ill-equipped foot soldiers against a vast army with nine hundred iron chariots! Read Psalm 20:7–8.

Do you ever find yourself looking with fear and trembling at a mountainous obstacle in front of you? What do you do? Check all that apply.

_______ Seek another person to go with you
_______ Look for reasons why you should not go forward
_______ Pray to be excused from this challenge
_______ Go in confidence that "if the Lord is for us, who can be against us?" (Romans 8:31)
_______ Other

What battle or obstacle are you facing? Prepare for yourself a battle plan. [1]Identify the enemy. [2]Pray for guidance and protection. [3]Trust in God's promises. [4]Read and believe the corresponding verses. [5]Act in faith. If your enemy is listed below, read the corresponding verse and take it to heart:

Satan—Colossians 2:15
Pride—Ephesians 2:9–10
Doubt—1 John 3:1
Hate—Ephesians 4:32
Apathy—Titus 2:14

Guilt—1 Corinthians 1:7–9
Hopelessness—Romans 8:38–39
Greed—Philippians 3:8
Fear—Romans 8:15
Unbelief—Mark 9:24

Write Deborah's words in Judges 4:9. ______________________________________________
________________________________________________________________________
________________________________________________________________________

Who would defeat Sisera? ________________ Through whose hands? ________________

Barak summoned the men from Zebulun and Naphtali together, and ten thousand men went up with him. "Deborah also went up with him" (Judges 4:10).

Keep your boots on, because tomorrow, we will witness a battle that belongs to the Lord.

## Discussion Question

Discuss the solution to the battle that rages within each of us according to Romans 7:23, 25.

## Personal Application Question

How do you find strength to go forward when you see the opposition but know that the Lord is with you?

Take a few minutes to write a prayer based on Psalm 20:7–8.

## Day Four

# The Battle Belongs to the Lord

I will sing praise to the Lord, the God of Israel.
—Judges 5:3

The Lord did an amazing thing the night before the battle. He sent a torrent of rain so that the Kishon River flooded its banks. In the morning, Deborah urged Barak, "Arise! For this is the day in which the Lord has given Sisera into your hands; behold, the Lord has gone out before you." (Judges 4:14)

With the flooding came mud and muck. The chariots were rendered useless; even the horses stamped the ground in their effort to escape (Judges 5:21–22). (A similar thing happened when Napoleon defeated the Turks in the same place in AD 1799.)

All those in the army of Sisera were killed by the sword; not one escaped except Sisera. He fled on foot and ran to the tent of Heber with his wife, Jael, "for there was peace between Jabin, the king of Canaan who ruled in Hazor, and the house of Heber." (Heber the Kenite had separated himself from the Kenites—from the sons of the father-in-law of Moses—and pitched his tent near Kedesh.) (Judges 1:16, 4:11)

Read Judges 4:18–20. What impression do you have of Jael? ______________________________

Instead of giving Sisera protection, what did Jael do? See Judges 4:21–22. ____________________
______________________________________________________________________________

Read Deborah's poetic version of the same incident found in Judges 5:26–27. Do you think Deborah was surprised that a woman, Jael, killed the greatest commander of the enemy army? See Judges 4:4, 9. ____________________

Why or why not?____________________

____________________

____________________

____________________

Are you even a little amazed that the Lord God would call a *woman* to do such an act of bravery? ____________ Therefore, who do you think received the glory? ______________ To whom did Deborah give the praise? (Judges 5:1–2) ____________________

When you are faced with insurmountable odds, do you wait in anticipation for the Lord to act on your behalf? "From of old no one has heard or perceived by the ear, no eye has seen a God besides you, who acts for those who wait for him" (Isaiah 64:4). Read 2 Corinthians 12:9.

The land had peace for forty years under Deborah's rule as judge over Israel prior to her death. Several other judges ruled over Israel, including Gideon and Samson. After every judge died, the people of Israel would do evil in the sight of the Lord, and the Lord would again deliver them into the hands of their enemies. After one such time of affliction, the people of Israel cried out to be delivered. What was the Lord's response to one such outcry as found in Judges 10:13–14? ____________________

____________________

____________________

The people of Israel confessed their sin, put away their foreign gods, and cried out to be delivered once again. After the Lord recapped the many times He had delivered the sons of Israel from Egypt and from the hands of their many enemies, the Lord "could bear the misery of Israel no longer" (Judges 10:16). So once again, He delivered the people of Israel under Judge Japhthah.

Judges 17:6 and 21:25 appropriately summarize the era of judges: "There was no king to rule over Israel and everyone did what was right in his own eyes." Left to ourselves with no governing body, man always seems to run amuck, don't you agree?

## Discussion Questions

In Deborah's position as judge over Israel, why was it so important for her to trust in the Lord? What influence does a leader who trusts in the Lord have over a nation? Give examples.

## Personal Application Question

How do you confront your fears, seek to lay them aside, and strive to take up the courage to do what you are called to do?

Take a few minutes to write a prayer, asking God for an added measure of faith in order to trust and obey Him as He calls you to make a difference in the life of another, or in your family, or in your church, or in your community.

## Day Five

# Learning from Deborah

Be still, and know that I am God; I will be exalted among
the nations, I will be exalted in the earth.
—Psalm 46:10

Trust in the Lord with all your heart and do no lean on your own understanding.
—Proverbs 3:5

God is Israel's true Savior. Deborah recognized this fact. She believed it. She lived it. Many times, the people of Israel realized it, and many times they did not (and still do not) accept it. Read the words of Tikva Frymer-Kensky.

> On Mount Tabor, Deborah the prophet announces the victory. She herself does not go down to the battle. Like Moses, Deborah is not a battle commander. Her role is to inspire, predict, and celebrate in song. Her weapon is the word, and her very name is an anagram of "she spoke" (Dibberah). The battle itself is not essential. It is important only to remember that God fought: God distressed Sisera. Deborah has announced God's victory, Barak has facilitated it, and God has saved Israel. The Song of Deborah provides a glimpse of how God defeated Canaan: God brought a flash flood that made a bog of sliding mud in which chariots were useless.[1] See Judges 5.

It is not probable that Deborah and Jael, the woman who drove the tent peg through the temple of Sisera, killing Sisera in his sleep, were even acquainted with one another, but God wove their lives together in a most amazing way. In one instance, the Lord commanded a *woman,* Deborah, to give the battle cry. In the same battle, the Lord brought into play another *woman,* Jael, who was instrumental in the victory of the Israelites against the Canaanites.

"Jael being a woman, is a further sign that Yahweh ultimately is responsible for the victory: The mighty Canaanite general Sisera will be 'sold' by the Lord into the hand of a woman—the ultimate degradation" (Judges 4:9).[2]

God accomplished His purpose through men and women in profound ways that give undeniable evidence that He is sovereign. When I think of a modern woman who was instrumental in the shaping of Israel, Golda Meir immediately comes to mind. Always concerned with her people, she worked tirelessly to help ensure protection of European Jews. In 1948, Golda Meir was part of the People's Council signing the proclamation establishing the State of Israel.

What does God require of *us* in order for us to be called of God? Write Psalm 46:10. ___________

_______________________________________________________________

What must *we* do to be effective servants of the Lord God Almighty? Write Proverbs 3:5. _______

_______________________________________________________________

_______________________________________________________________

What if someone is a cashier at a discount store, a mother of a handicapped child or of healthy children, an office worker, a student, a resident in a nursing home, a hospital worker, or in any number of other situations in life? Does that mean that God does not have a specific calling on her life? To the contrary, God is the one who has placed each one of us in the exact position we may find ourselves unless we have been disobedient to Him. Most of us will never attain a position of prestige, but that does not make our calling any less important.

The following statement by commentator Chuck Smith bears repeating. When we find ourselves in a place where we think we have cause to grumble and to complain, we must remember, "For God is the One who has brought me to these circumstances. God is the One who has placed me here, unless I've been disobedient to Him."[3] The same holds true for wherever and whatever circumstance we may be in—whether prestigious or ordinary. We are here by God's design and calling. Keep in mind that we are exactly where we are supposed to be, doing precisely what He calls us to be doing, *unless* we've been disobedient to Him. Be encouraged that in the grand scheme of things, we are where we are supposed to be.

Deborah has set a beautiful example for us as an obedient, trusting woman of faith in her calling as judge over Israel; she brought glory and honor to the God she served. I hope you enjoyed our time with Deborah as much as I did. Remember, our greatest calling is to glorify Jesus Christ, and we bring glory to the Father when we trust Him in all things.

## Discussion Question

Discuss the difference between "being in an unpleasant situation that entices grumbling" and "envying a position that sparks jealousy" using Hebrews 13:5 as a backdrop. ("Keep your lives free from the love of money and be content with what you have, because God has said, 'Never will I leave you; never will I forsake you.'")

## Personal Application Question

Apply this verse to yourself: "When they saw the courage of Peter and John and realized that they were unschooled, ordinary men, they were astonished and they took note that these men had been with Jesus" (Acts 4:13).

Take a few minutes to write a prayer, asking God to help you be a witness of His glory in your ordinary, everyday life.

[1]Frymer-Kensky, Tikva. *Victors, Victims, Virgins, and Voice: Rereading the Women of the Bible. New York, n.d.)*

[2]Coogan, Michael D. *A Brief Introduction to the Old Testament: The Hebrew Bible in its Context* (London: Oxford University Press, 2009), 180.

[3]Smith, Chuck, *Exodus 16-18* (Costa Mesa, CA: The Word For Today, 2000)

# Week Seven
# When Evil Strikes Within

## Day One

# Tamar—Princess in the Palace

Arise, anoint him; for this is he.
—1 Samuel 16:12

Before we greet Tamar, let's meet her father. David shepherded his father's sheep in Bethlehem and was the youngest of his seven brothers. He was handsome and had beautiful eyes, and as a teenage lad, he was chosen to reign as king over Israel.

David did not seek to be king; he didn't have to. He was called by God and anointed by Samuel, the prophet. The Lord said to Samuel, "Arise, anoint him; for this is he" (1 Samuel 16:12). But David did not become king at that time; he had to wait until he was thirty years old. In the meantime, he served Saul, the first king over Israel. Since David was a skilled musician, he played the harp and sang for Saul when Saul was troubled with bouts of depression. David also became a mighty warrior—a man of valor. He succeeded in all he did, "for the LORD God of hosts was with him" (2 Samuel 5:10).

Even Abner, commander in Saul's army, said, "For the Lord has spoken of David, saying, 'By the hand of My servant David I will save My people Israel from the hand of the Philistines and from the hand of all their enemies'" (2 Samuel 3:18, NASB).

On another occasion, the Lord said to David, "You will shepherd My people Israel, and you will be a ruler over Israel" (2 Samuel 5:2, NASB). David knew he was chosen to be king, but for about thirteen years, through many battles, victories, threats on his life, and escapes, he served Saul faithfully.

David was thirty years old when Saul, wounded and dying, fell on his own sword during one of many battles. How did David react to the news that Saul was dead? See 2 Samuel 1:11–12. ___________

___

___

It came about afterward that David inquired of the Lord. What did he ask? See 2 Samuel 2:1. ____

___

David settled in the cities of Hebron, and there the men of Judah anointed David king over the house of Judah, but Ish-bosheth, Saul's son, reigned over Israel. When Ish-bosheth was killed in battle, all the people of Israel came to David and anointed him king over Israel as well.

David established his capital in neutral territory between Israel and Judah—in Jerusalem, the city of David. David reigned forty years—seven and half years over Judah and thirty-three years over Israel and Judah (2 Samuel 5:4–5). What kind of king was David? See 2 Samuel 8:15. ______________

___

___

David reigned over his people doing what was just and right. In comparison, Isaiah 9:7 says of Jesus Christ, "There will be no end to the increase of His government or of peace, on the throne of David and over his kingdom, to establish it and to uphold it with justice and righteousness from then on and forevermore."

Again, Isaiah foretold, "But with righteousness He (Jesus Christ) will judge the poor, and decide with fairness for the afflicted of the earth … Also righteousness will be the belt about His loins and faithfulness the belt about His waist" (Isaiah 11:4). The Lord of hosts will accomplish this.

By this time, David had married Michal, Saul's daughter. He had also married Ahinoam and Abigail. He also took more wives and concubines, which was in direct violation of Deuteronomy 17:17, which clearly spelled out the conditions of a king over Israel: [1]to be chosen by God, [2]to be an Israelite, [3]not to imitate royal courts of other nations in his desire for horses, wives, and money, and [4]to have a copy of the Law and obey it. But in ancient times, international alliances were often sealed by the marriage of a king's daughter to the other participant in the treaty. It would not be politically correct in our day! David had many sons and daughters; his oldest son was named Amnon. Tuck this name in the front of your memory, as Amnon plays an important role in our study.

David also married Maachah, daughter of Talmai, king of the neighboring kingdom of Geshur. He had two children with Maachah—Absalom, his third-oldest son, and Tamar. "Now in all Israel was no one as handsome as Absalom, so highly praised; from the sole of his foot to the crown of his head there was no defect in him" (2 Samuel 14:25).

If we could listen to Tamar speaking about herself, she may have said words to this effect: "It was said of me that my mother's beauty was given me as a gift, but I discovered it was not a gift to be cherished for it has become a snare and a burden for me."[1]

Tamar's heritage was one of royalty. Her father was King David, and her mother was the daughter of a king, making Tamar daughter of one king and a granddaughter of another king. Tamar truly was a princess in the palace, but that did not protect her from an unspeakable tragedy that changed her life forever, as we shall see tomorrow.

## Discussion Question

What are some advantages and disadvantages of being born with a silver spoon in one's mouth?

## Personal Application Question

If you met someone of high position—politically, socially, or economically—what do you think your actions would show? Check all that apply.

| | | |
|---|---|---|
| _______ great respect | _______ nervousness | _______ embarrassment |
| _______ indifference | _______ awe/amazement | _______ critical attitude |
| _______ envy | _______ other | |

What would your actions show if you met a dirty and smelly homeless person?

| | | |
|---|---|---|
| _______ great respect | _______ nervousness | _______ embarrassment |
| _______ indifference | _______ awe/amazement | _______ critical attitude |
| _______ envy | _______ other | |

Were your responses similar? Are you surprised?

Take a few minutes to write a prayer, asking God to help you to not be a respecter of positions but rather one who loves the person.

## *Notes*

[1] Kroon, Rita. *Letters from the Past* (Denver, Colorado: Outskirts Press, 2011), 114.

## Day Two

# Silent Cries

I have sunk in deep mire and there is no foothold.
—Psalm 69:2

Let's meet part of Tamar's family. Tamar and Absalom were brother and sister—children of Maacha and King David. Absalom was third-oldest of the king's many sons. Tamar also had many half-brothers. Amnon was the oldest—the firstborn of the king. Amnon had a very unnatural and unreciprocated attraction for Tamar. Tamar is described in 2 Samuel 13:1-2 as ____________ and ______________________________________________.

Amnon thought he loved Tamar, but in actuality, he *lusted,* for her even though incest was as strictly forbidden in their culture in first-century BC as it is in our culture today. Second Samuel 13:2 says, "And Amnon was so frustrated (sexually) because of his sister Tamar that he made himself ______, for she was a virgin and it seemed hard to Amnon to do anything to her."

Beloved, I want to be extremely sensitive and very tenderhearted to those of you who may have been deeply wounded—victimized by a perpetrator either sexually, verbally, emotionally, or physically—and I certainly do not want to cause undue heartache or stir up painful memories. On the contrary, I hope today's lesson will lend encouragement and bring healing as we pursue a very tragic and life-changing event in Tamar's life.

If asked, Tamar may have spoken of Amnon with these words: "Several times, I have noticed that he looks at me strangely. I know it is not my imagination that he seems to wait in places where I pass by.

His looks betray an unnatural interest in me that makes me feel grateful for the women and guards that always accompany me."[1]

What evidence of virginity were daughters of the king required to wear? (2 Samuel 13:18)

____________________________________________________________

____________________________________________________________

Amnon had a shrewd and unscrupulous cousin named Jonadab. On one particular day, Jonadab asked Amnon, "O son of the king, why are you so depressed morning after morning?" (2 Samuel 13:4) Write Amnon's reply from the same verse. ____________________________

____________________________________________________________

____________________________________________________________

It didn't take but a few seconds for Jonadab (without a shred of conscience) to come up with a plan that would allow Amnon to have his way with Tamar. Describe his plan according to 2 Samuel 13:5.

____________________________________________________________

____________________________________________________________

Amnon feigned his illness so well that he fooled everyone—even the king!

Who unwittingly helped Amnon carry out his diabolical plan? (2 Samuel 13:7) _______________

Read 2 Samuel 13:8–10. How do you suppose Tamar might have felt? Check all that apply.

______ fearful
______ unaware of the danger
______ wanting to obey her father
______ happy to serve her ill half-brother
______ important, because she was called
______ unsuspecting
______ eager to please
______ other

Amnon ordered all the servants out of the room and then commanded Tamar to "bring the food into my bedroom" (2 Samuel 13:9–10). It was at this point that Amnon grabbed Tamar and forced himself upon her, violating her as she struggled and pleaded in vain. We can only surmise the terrifying scene, since the Scriptures discreetly and wisely omit the details.

I cannot even begin to put into words, given a similar scenario, how I think I would have felt or what I would have tried to do to protect myself, but I think it would have been fairly close to what Tamar must have felt and what she must have tried to do to defend herself, wouldn't you agree? Her rape evokes great empathy for her; does it not for you as well? We need not focus on the actual rape but rather on what happened afterward.

What immediate effect did this act have on Amnon? (2 Samuel 13:15)________________________

________________________________________________________________________________

How commonplace for lust, once gratified, to turn to hate! Rapists have nothing more than hostility and disdain for those they have victimized; they care nothing at all for the irreparable harm they have caused to another human being. And that is exactly what Amnon felt for Tamar! Listen to Amnon's words to his young male attendant in 2 Samuel 13:17: "Now throw this woman out of my presence, and lock the door behind her."

Throw this woman out? Compare his reference to Tamar with 2 Samuel 13:6, where he said, "Please let my sister, Tamar, come and make me a couple of cakes." Do you hear his disdain for Tamar after his attack?

What did Tamar do? (2 Samuel 13:19)____________________________________________

________________________________________________________________________________

Tamar was clearly traumatized, wailing and tearing her clothes as she ran. There were no police to call, no one to comfort her, and no one to come to her aid. She was alone in her despair. She was desperate in her need.

How ironic that King David should have previously written these words during his own despair in persecution that so aptly describe the reproach of Tamar and are recorded in Psalm 69:

> I have sunk in deep mire! There is no foothold. I have come into deep waters, and a flood overflows me. I am weary with my crying; my throat is parched. Those who hate me without a cause are more than the hairs of my head. Those who would destroy me are powerful. Dishonor has covered my face. I have become estranged from my brothers and as an alien to my brothers. I wept in my soul and it became my reproach. I made sackcloth of my clothing and I became a byword to those who sit in the gate who talk about me. I am the song of the drunkards. Reproach has broken my heart. I look for sympathy, but there was none; and for comforters, I have found none.

Of course, we all want the wicked to be punished with a punishment that fits the crime, right? And certainly the punishment is to be swift, wouldn't you agree? Think about this—if you were the one victimized, would you want the perpetrator to be punished according to man's law or according to God's standard of justice? Why? ________________________________________________

________________________________________________________________________________

________________________________________________________________________________

What if the evil one did not seem to receive any disciplinary action at all while the one who was victimized suffered mental anguish, guilt, shame, and emotional derailment? Beloved, do you not know that the evil one will stand before a righteous judge and give an account of his every deed? His punishment will certainly fit the evil done to the innocent. What does Romans 14:12 say? _______

______________________________________________________________________

______________________________________________________________________

Read Psalm 11:5–7.

Tomorrow we will watch as further hurtful events unfold for the wounded and broken Tamar.

## Discussion Question

Discuss the proper response that God seeks from us when bad things happen to good people. Think about the greatest injustice done to any human being. Could there be any greater atrocity done to man than the cruel torture and shameful crucifixion of Jesus Christ?

## Personal Application Question

If there has been evil committed against us personally or against one of our loved ones, we must leave the vengeance to the Lord. *"Never take your own revenge, beloved, but leave room for the wrath of God, for it is written, 'Vengeance is Mine, I will repay,' says the Lord."* (Romans 12:19) Have you or anyone you know who has been victimized overcome the justifiable anger against the perpetrator of a heinous offense and experienced true forgiveness? Explain.

Take a few minutes to write a prayer, imploring God to give you an abundance of His grace to even begin the process of seeking to forgive someone who may have wounded you or your loved one beyond description—whether that person seeks forgiveness or not.

[1] Kroon, Rita. *Letters from the Past* (Denver, Colorado: Outskirts Press, 2011), 114.

Day Three

# Wounded and Broken

A bruised reed He will not break, and a dimly burning wick He will not extinguish.
—Isaiah 42:3

Yesterday, we watched in horror as Tamar fled from the bedroom of her half-brother after being raped. Amidst her tears, loud cries, and torn clothing, she ran into her brother, Absalom.

"Has Amnon your brother been with you?" Absalom asked. Tamar could only stand there with her hand on her head, sobbing. What shocking words did Absalom say to Tamar?
(2 Samuel 13:20)____________________________________________________________
__________________________________________________________________________

Keep silent? Pretend this never happened? Don't do anything rash? What about Leviticus 20:17, which says, "If there is a man who takes his sister, his father's daughter or his mother's daughter, so that he sees her nakedness and she sees his nakedness, it is a disgrace; and they shall be cut off in the sight of the sons of their people"? What about Deuteronomy 27:22, which says, "Cursed is he who lies with his sister, the daughter of his father or of his mother"? Absalom did take Tamar into his home, where she remained in seclusion, but nothing was done to Amnon.

Absalom quieted the matter for the time being, determining in his mind a plot to take revenge against Amnon when he least expected it (2 Samuel 3:22, 32).

Did King David know of the rape? (2 Samuel 13:21) __________________ What was his response?
__________________________________________________________________________

Why do you think he did not vindicate his daughter's rape? ______________________________

________________________________________________________________________

For a possible clue, let's go back to the time King David had his infamous adulterous affair with Bathsheba. When Nathan, the prophet, confronted David regarding his sin, David said, "I have sinned against the Lord" (2 Samuel 12:13). David confessed his sin with true godly sorrow taking full responsibility for his actions and sin against the Lord.

The Lord forgave David. "However, because of that deed (the adulterous affair, impregnating Bathsheba, and having her husband killed in battle), you (David) have given occasion to the enemies of the Lord to blaspheme. Therefore, the child also that is born to you (and Bathsheba) shall surely die," Nathan said (2 Samuel 12:14). His infant son surely did die, and David grieved deeply. He loved his son, and it was because of his own actions that his infant son had died! Do you feel his anguish?

Could it be that David did nothing to Amnon, his firstborn, for the rape of Tamar because the punishment would have meant death for Amnon according to Leviticus 20:17? What if David remembered his own adulterous affair with Bathsheba? Even though he repented, was forgiven, and was spared death from his sexual immorality, did he think he could rightfully inflict punishment on Amnon? (2 Samuel 12:13) Whatever the reason, Tamar was left desolate.

How did Absalom respond to Amnon? (2 Samuel 13:22)______________________________
________________________________________________ For how long? (2 Samuel 13:23)
________________________________________________________________________

Tamar was devastated—a desolate woman. Webster's dictionary defines *desolate* as "left alone; lonely; solitary." There is no evidence that indicates that Tamar was ever anything but a desolate woman for the rest of her life. Tamar was judged and ostracized by family and friends for something that was not her fault, but Psalm 34:15–22 leads me to believe that Tamar was comforted by the Lord Himself; wouldn't you agree? Write the words of Psalm 34:15–22, and let the meaning of those verses sink deeply into your soul. ________________________________________________

________________________________________________________________________

________________________________________________________________________

________________________________________________________________________

________________________________________________________________________

________________________________________________________________________

________________________________________________________________________

________________________________________________________________________

________________________________________________________________________

________________________________________________________________________

Meanwhile, Absalom burned with hatred and plotted revenge against Amnon for violating his sister.

Tomorrow we will witness the dire consequences of seeking revenge rather than pursuing justice.

## Discussion Question

Discuss the traumatic effects of those victimized by *non-physical* violence, such as verbal, emotional, or psychological abuse and the laws, or lack thereof, pertaining to such abuse.

## Personal Application Question

What counsel and comfort would you give to someone who has been victimized, and what would you base that on?

Take a few minutes to read and pray this prayer according to Isaiah 41:10: "Father in heaven, I pray that my friend would fear not nor be dismayed. I ask that you would strengthen her, that you would help her, that you would uphold her with your righteous right hand. Reveal yourself as her God—a very present help in the time of trouble."[1]

## *Notes*

[1] Kroon, Rita. *Praying the Scriptures* (Denver, Colorado: Outskirts Press, 2011), 15.

## Day Four

# Consequences

"Vengeance is Mine. I will repay," says the Lord.
—Romans 12:19

Did Absalom have ulterior motives when he plotted revenge against Amnon? After all, Amnon was the firstborn and would be expected to inherit the throne. Could there have been jealous rivalry between the two half-brothers? Was Absalom secretly planning to take over the kingdom? Did he see this as his opportunity to get rid of one who stood in the way of his quest? Read Psalm 94:11.

Plotting revenge can become an all-consuming fire and is always a dangerous thing. Unforgiveness is as equally destructive as plotting revenge and can victimize the wounded again and again with bitterness and hatred, making any healing humanly impossible to attain. Write Ephesians 4:31–32.

________________________________________

________________________________________

________________________________________

________________________________________

It came about after two years that Absalom celebrated the sheep shearing—a day of prosperity—and invited all the king's sons, including Amnon, to go to the festive occasion. When "Amnon's heart was merry with wine" (2 Samuel 13:28), Absalom commanded his servants to kill Amnon and "not to fear; have not I myself commanded you?" So the servants carried out the orders and killed Amnon.

When the rest of the king's sons saw this, they fled. I'm certain they must have thought they were next to being killed. Rumor raced back to King David that all his sons were dead. But what message did Jonadab relate to the king? (2 Samuel 13:32)______________________________

____________________________________________________________

Remember, this is the same Jonadab who devised the plot for Amnon to feign illness in order to get Tamar to his bedroom. Notice that Jonadab did not involve himself in the ploy, however, but rather turned the spotlight onto Absalom.

What did Absalom do? (2 Samuel 13:34)____________________________________

How did David respond to the news of Amnon's death? (2 Samuel 13:36)________________

____________________________________________________________

What does it mean to you to *weep very bitterly?* ________________________________

____________________________________________________________

Tamar might possibly have felt vindicated, except that Amnon's death was not for the crime he had committed against her. It was because of revenge, not justice. Consequently, turmoil erupted in the kingdom.

Absalom was gone for three years before King David's commander was allowed to bring Absalom back to Jerusalem. Another two years passed, but King David would not allow his son into his presence, even though Absalom repeatedly asked Joab, the commander, to arrange an audience with his father. Because Joab would not arrange the meeting, Absalom's revenge mode took over once again, and Absalom burned Joab's barley fields.

Finally, the meeting was arranged between King David and his son, Absalom. David kissed Absalom, which signified that Absalom was restored to favor with his father. During the five years of separation from David, however, Absalom had grown bitter, resulting in Absalom planning a revolt against his father, the king. He craftily stole the hearts of the people away from the king (2 Samuel 15:6). What did Absalom secretly gather for himself? (2 Samuel 15:1) ________________, ____________, and ____________________________________________________

What tactic did Absalom use to sway the allegiance of the men of Jerusalem to himself? See 2 Samuel 15:2–4. __________________________________________________

____________________________________________________________

____________________________________________________________

Did it work? (2 Samuel 15:12) ________________________________________

After several years of strategizing, what did Absalom tell the king was his reason for wanting to leave town? (2 Samuel 15:7–8)____________________________________________

______________________________________________________________________

The unsuspecting king said, "________________________________________" (2 Samuel15:9). Read 2 Samuel 15:11. There is a dangerous risk when people jump on someone else's bandwagon without knowing facts, wouldn't you agree? These two hundred men got themselves into a deadly conflict between Absalom and King David.

Absalom not only stirred up the men of Jerusalem, but also sent spies throughout all the tribes of Israel, saying, "As soon as you hear the sound of the trumpet, then you shall say, 'Absalom is king in Hebron.'" (2 Samuel 15:10) Remember, Hebron is where King David first began his rule as king after the death of Saul.

Does it not seem obvious to you that Absalom wanted more than revenge for Amnon violating his sister, Tamar? At what point did this become an apparent quest for power? ____________________

______________________________________________________________________

Absalom's revenge for Tamar's rape escalated into premeditated murder, rebellion, lying, dishonoring David as king, greed, deception, hypocrisy, and revolt. Absalom had wrong motives from the start, and his self-deception led him down a deadly path.

Of course, we cannot see what the future holds, but this account was recorded for our learning so that we are made aware that certain *patterns* of wrong behavior always lead to destruction in one way or another.

When word of the imminent revolt reached the king, what did he do? (2 Samuel 15:14) __________ ____________________________________ and all the people of his household and the city went with him. David fled for his life and for fear of an attack on Jerusalem if he remained in the city. Perhaps he was seeking to avert civil war and the bloodshed of hundreds of innocent people.

Absalom and his men pursued David and his men. David placed commanders over thousands and commanders over hundreds. What command did David *repeatedly* give to his commanders as recorded in 2 Samuel 18:5, 12? __________________________________________________

What mercy! Even after all the evil Absalom had done, David showed love and mercy. But the men did not, and Absalom was killed.

Read David's response to the news of Absalom's death in 2 Samuel 18:33, 19:4.

I am reminded of the words to the song "My Savior, My God": "I am not skilled to understand what God has willed—what God has planned. I only know at His right hand stands One who is my Savior."

We say goodbye to Tamar and trust that she found comfort in God through words written by her father that were set to music that soothed the soul. We are also reminded of the atrocities done on earth from the beginning of time, and we join with the apostle John in saying, "Amen! Come Lord Jesus" (Revelation 22:20, NASB).

## Discussion Question

Do you think people, in general, are easily persuaded of their discontent by leaders, politically, spiritually, or in the workplace? Why is it dangerous to sow seeds of discontent based on an individual vendetta? Read Ephesians 4:29.

## Personal Application Question

When you hear comments from a disgruntled person, what are you more apt to do? Check all that apply.

_______ check out the source of contention
_______ agree, adding your own comments
_______ find others who agree or disagree
_______ side with the disgruntled person
_______ offer a workable solution privately
_______ do nothing
_______ defend the offended
_______ argue
_______ walk away
_______ other

Take a few minutes to write a prayer based on Philippians 4:6–7.

## Day Five

# Comfort from a Reliable Source

A broken and contrite heart, O God, You will not despise.
—Psalm 51:17

"I am weary with my crying and my throat is parched." (Psalm 69:3) "I would have despaired unless I had believed that I would see the goodness of the Lord in the land of the living" (Psalm 27:13)). When one is devastated by shame, guilt, grief, or heartache, where is there respite? Where is there comfort? "From whence comes my help?" (Psalm 121:1) Write the answer to the question found in Psalm 121:2. ______________________________

______________________________

When a person is victimized, he or she is often labeled. For instance, Tamar may have been labeled "the rape victim." Labeling one who has been victimized only adds a negative identification to that person and continues holding him or her in bondage. Hurtful labels can isolate and imprison one as much as physical seclusion does. It is better to say that Tamar was raped, but she was still a young woman worthy of compassion, tender care, and loving arms. Seek the Lord as you help begin the process of healing one devastated by rape or any other extreme abuse of the body, mind, or soul. Seek professional counseling. Reassure the one victimized that the abuse was not his or her fault. Come alongside the one who was victimized. Validate the person and his or her feelings as you lead the person to the one who "will wipe away every tear from their eyes, and death shall be no more, neither shall there be mourning, nor crying, nor pain anymore, for the former things have passed away" (Revelation 21:4, ESV), Remember to pray, pray, pray.

Psalm 69 goes on to say, "You who seek God, let your heart revive. For the Lord hears the needy, and does not despise His who are prisoners."

Since David was the author of many psalms, the words of these psalms may very well have been sung, accompanied by stringed instruments, within Tamar's hearing. "A broken and contrite heart, O God, you will not despise" (Psalm 51:17).

Being victimized by rape leaves one feeling dirty and worthless. A repentant sinner may feel the same uncleanness, but our heavenly Father cleanses us and turns our darkness into light. "Purify me with hyssop, and I shall be clean; wash me, and I shall be whiter than snow. Make me to hear joy and gladness" (Psalm 51:7–8). There is hope for healing! There is freedom in forgiving!

Forgiveness does not necessarily mean a restored relationship (if there was one previously), but it does mean freeing oneself from becoming victimized again. Becoming victimized by the bitterness, hatred, and anger toward the perpetrator may incapacitate a person almost as much as the perpetrated crime does.

Beloved, do not let your past dictate who you are; let it be part of who you will become!

## Discussion Question

What would you do if you knew of a friend who was traumatized in one way or another and did not want to talk about it, since the wound was too deep or the shame too great? If you sense that she is being crushed by the burden, what would be a sensitive and appropriate way for you to help her begin the healing process? Review Psalm 34:15–22.

## Personal Application Question

If you have been victimized, how did you handle the situation?

_______ go into denial
_______ harbor anger
_______ become indifferent
_______ seek the Lord in prayer
_______ join a support group
_______ talk openly
_______ plan revenge
_______ become depressed
_______ seek counseling
_______ become a recluse
_______ become an advocate for those victimized
_______ other

How would you handle it differently now?

Take a few minutes and write your own psalm, expressing to the Lord what is on your heart. Include praise to the Lord for His care and concern and His love for you based on Proverbs 18:10.

# Week Eight
# Poetic Justice

## Day One
## Esther—Captive in Persia

## Day Two
## The Plot Thickens

## Day Three
## Poetic Justice

## Day Four
## A New Edict

## Day Five
## Virtue Reigns

Day One

# Esther—Captive in Persia

Let beautiful young virgins be sought for the king.
—Esther 2:2

The woman we will meet today is Esther, and the account of her life is found in the book named after her. The book of Esther covers a ten-year portion (483–473 BC) of the reign of Xerxes I.

The heritage of God's chosen nation, Israel, is one of blessing and woe, peace and war, but Israelites were always a people of promise. When the Jews had been in captivity for seventy years in Babylon under King Nebuchadnezzar, Babylon was overthrown by Cyrus, King of Persia. The area under his control was from India to Ethiopia—present-day Pakistan and North Sudan. King Cyrus issued a decree allowing the displaced peoples to return to their homelands, and many did return, but for reasons unknown to us, many of the Jews remained in exile in Persia.[1] Esther was such an exile.

Esther was a young orphan girl who had been adopted by her older cousin, Mordecai, an honorable, caring, gentle man. (Esther was her Persian name; Hadassah was her Hebrew name.)

When Esther was about ten years old, a new king began his reign in Persia. His Greek name was Xerxes, but in Hebrew, he was called Ahasuerus. After a time, he lavishly displayed "the riches of his royal glory and the splendor of his great majesty" for an amazing six months! (Esther 1:4) All the princes of his provinces, the army officers, and the nobles attended this gala event.

At the conclusion, a seven-day drinking feast was held by the king for all the people who were present in Susa, the capital (Esther 1:5). It was on the last day of this banquet that the drunken king ordered

Queen Vashti to appear in her royal robes in order to parade her before the people so that they could see her beauty. What did Queen Vashti do? See Esther 1:12.____________________! In King Ahasuerus' anger and on the counsel of his wise men, the king divorced his beautiful queen. In addition, the king issued a decree that "every man should be the master in his own house" (Esther 1:22).

Can you imagine what it may have been like for a young Jewish girl growing up in a land where there was a king and a queen? Perhaps she had a fairytale dream of becoming a beautiful queen herself, wearing royal robes and exquisite jewels fit only for a queen. Perhaps Esther had such an imagination. Could the divorce of her beautiful queen have crushed her dreams of the splendor of being a queen? Do you remember childhood dreams of make-believe? What were your dreams, and how have they changed as you have matured? ______________________________

________________________________________________

________________________________________________

In time, the king remembered Queen Vashti with sadness. To console the king, his attendants suggested, "Let beautiful young virgins be sought for the king" and "let the young lady who pleases the king be queen in place of Vashti." (Esther 2:2) And so the decree went out that all the beautiful young virgins be brought to the palace and placed in the harem.

As a teenage girl, Esther was also brought before the king. Mordecai had instructed Esther not to reveal her Jewish nationality, and Esther obeyed (Esther 2:10).

After a year of beautification with oil of myrrh, spices, and the cosmetics for the women, each young lady would be brought to the king but would not go into the king's presence again unless she pleased the king and was summoned by name. When it was Esther's turn to be brought before the king, what happened? (Esther 2:9)

What did Mordecai do?
See Esther 2:11. ________________

________________

How often? ________________
What does this say about the character of Mordecai? ________________

________________

________________

How do you think Esther felt, knowing that her father-figure cousin was watching over her?

________________

How does it make you feel to know that our heavenly Father watches over us with His perfect love? ________________

Proverbs 2:7–8 says that God not only watches over us, but He also stores up sound wisdom for the upright. He is a shield to those who walk in integrity, guarding the paths of justice, and He preserves the way of His godly ones.

Write Proverbs 18:10. ________________

________________

________________

Esther was taken to the royal palace of King Ahasuerus in the tenth month in the seventh year of his reign (Esther 2:16). How did the king respond? See Esther 2:17. ________________

________________

What did the king do to honor Esther? (Esther 2:17) ________________

________________

One day, as Mordecai sat in the palace gate, he overheard two gatekeepers plot to kill King Ahasuerus. He sent word immediately to Esther, urging her to tell the king. Of course, Esther obeyed Mordecai, as was her usual manner while she was in his care. The plot was investigated and found to be true.

The incident was written in the presence of the king in the book of the Chronicles of the Kings of Media and Persia (Esther 2:23).

We take leave of Esther in the palace until tomorrow, when we will see justice served as a direct result of this incident.

## Discussion Question

King Ahasuerus and Queen Vashti did not have an ideal godly marriage. Discuss God's ideal husband/wife relationship based on Ephesians 5:33 and Colossians 3:18–19.

## Personal Application Question

If your marriage is less than a godly marriage, what can and should you do to remain faithful to the Lord based on 1 Peter 3:1–7?

Take a few minutes to write a prayer, asking God to increase your confidence in His love and care of your life. Ask God to show you who may be going through a season of disappointment, trouble, or trial and could be encouraged by you.

[1] Kroon, Rita. *Letters from the Past* (Denver, Colorado: Outskirts Press, 2011), 129.

## Day Two

# The Plot Thickens

Who knows whether you have not attained royalty for such a time as this?
—Esther 4:14

After the hanging of the two would-be assassins and more than four years after Esther had been made queen, King Ahasuerus promoted a spiteful and egotistical man named Haman to be in authority over all the princes. (Haman was possibly related to the Amalekites [1 Samuel 15:8], and if so, Haman was a descendant of Esau, an enemy of the descendants of Jacob.) At the king's command, all the servants at the king's gate were to bow down and pay *homage* to Haman, which was a divine honor claimed by Persian kings.

Haman soon became puffed up with pride, so when Mordecai did not bow down to him, Haman became infuriated! The servants certainly noticed and asked Mordecai, "Why are you transgressing the king's command?" (Esther 3:3) In other words, "If we have to bow down to Haman, how come you don't have to?" What simple reason did Mordecai give to the servants after their daily questioning? (Esther 3:4)________________________________________________

____________________________________________________________

Haman realized that to kill only Mordecai would not solve his problem; he had to destroy *all* the Jews. An evil plan began to formulate in his mind, driving him to near madness as he set out to accomplish his plan. He wasted no time in going to the king. What did Haman say to the king? (Esther 3:8–9)

____________________________________________________________

____________________________________________________________

____________________________________________________________

In actuality, Haman was bribing the king, thinking he would use the money he would attain from killing the Jews to put into the king's treasury, but the king did not even bother to ask who these people were that had different laws and were disobeying the king's laws. King Ahasuerus simply gave Haman his signet ring "to do with them as you please" (Esther 3:11). What is Haman called in Esther 3:10? ______

It was on the thirteenth day of the *first* month that the king's scribes were summoned. Haman dictated the edict that was to go throughout all the provinces to destroy, kill, and annihilate all the Jews—young and old, women and children—on the thirteenth day of the *twelfth* month!

After Haman cold-heartedly issued a decree to annihilate the Jews, what is the very next thing he did and with whom? See Esther 4:15 ______

______

Meanwhile, what was going on in the city of Susa just outside the king's palace? See Esther 4:3. ___

______

To us, the edit for death would be like getting a diagnosis of a terminal illness that left us with only months to live and had no known cure, wouldn't you agree?

When Esther heard of the commotion in the city, she sent her attendant to Mordecai to learn what could cause such a stir and why. Mordecai told the attendant of the plan to destroy the Jews, and then he sent a copy of the edict with the attendant back to Esther and ordered her to plead with the king for her people. Esther's attendant now knew she was a Jewish woman. But that was not Esther's concern. What was her concern? (Esther 4:11) ______

______

______

Do you sense Esther's hesitation to obey Mordecai for the first time? ______
What did Mordecai respond? (Esther 4:13–14) ______

______

______

Mordecai reminded Esther that she risked death whether she approached the king or not.
Listen to his profound words found in Esther 4:14: "For if you remain silent at this time, relief and deliverance will arise for the Jews from another place and you and your father's house will perish. And who knows whether you have not attained royalty for such a time as this?" The realization that perhaps this was the reason that she, an orphaned Jewish girl, became queen over Persia penetrated her soul like a knife!

What significant request did Esther make of Mordecai? (Esther 4:16) ______

______

Esther would also fast with her maidens. For how long? ______________________________
This was an extremely serious situation, and Esther certainly did not take it lightly.

When you are faced with a major decision, how do you approach its resolution? ______________
______________________________________________________________________
______________________________________________________________________
______________________________________________________________________

What if it's not a life-or-death situation—how do you handle it? __________________________
______________________________________________________________________
______________________________________________________________________

"Be anxious for nothing, but in everything by prayer and supplication with thanksgiving let your requests be made known to God. And the peace of God, which surpasses all comprehension, shall guard your hearts and your minds in Christ Jesus" (Philippians 4:6–7). According to these verses, what should we be anxious about? ______________________________ In what things should we take our requests to the Lord? __________________________ How should we approach God? By ______________________ and ______________ with ___________________________. (Supplication is intense prayer—similar in intensity to what Esther prayed.) Once we have sought the Lord and made our need known to Him, what does God give us? __________________
What is said about the peace of God? __________________________________________ and
______________________________________________________________________
in ____________________________________________________________________

What secret did the apostle Paul discover for obtaining inner peace and strength in *every* circumstance? (Philippians 4:13)______________________________________________________
______________________________________________________________________

What words found in John 15:5 did Jesus say to convey the same meaning? ________________
______________________________________________________________________

Read the last few words of Esther 4:16. What does Esther say that indicated she put everything into the Lord's hands? " ______________________________________________________ "

After three days of fasting, Esther put on her royal robes and stood in the inner court of the king's palace, in front of the king's rooms, opposite to the entrance to the palace. How was she received? (Esther 5:2) ______________________________________________________________
What invitation did Esther give the king? (Esther 5:4) ____________________________________
______________________________________________________________________

At the banquet, as the king drank wine with Haman, the king asked Esther, "What is your petition?" Esther answered, "My petition and my request is: if I have found favor in the sight of the king, and if it please the king to grant my petition and do what I request may the king and Haman come to the banquet which I shall prepare for them tomorrow."

Esther may have lost her courage to expose Haman and his ruthless plot to kill the Jews, but it was *providential* that Esther planned a second banquet for the king and Haman the following day, for the intervening night proved to be quite a night for the king, Haman, and Mordecai.

Haman was glad and pleased of heart as he left the banquet—until he saw Mordecai, that is. As usual, Mordecai did not bow to Haman, which infuriated him immensely. But Haman controlled himself and went to his house. There, Haman bragged to his wife and his friends how only he and the king were invited by Queen Esther to a banquet. "Yet all of this does not satisfy me every time I see Mordecai the Jew sitting at the king's gate," Haman groaned (Esther 5:13).

What preposterous suggestion did Haman's wife offer? (Esther 5:14)______________________

______________________________________________________________________

That night, the king could not sleep, so he ordered that the book of the chronicles be read to him. When the king heard the account of Mordecai foiling the attempted assassination on his life, he asked what has been done to honor Mordecai. "Nothing," came the servants' reply (Esther 6:3).

The king asked his servants who was in the court; his servants replied that Haman was. For what reason had Haman entered the court of the king? (Esther 6:4) ______________________

______________________________________________________________________

______________________________________________________________________

The king said to bring Haman in. Naturally, the king stated his business before Haman could state his business. What did the king ask Haman? (Esther 6:6) ______________________

______________________________________________________________________

Of course, Haman thought the king was referring to him, so he suggested an elaborate public display of honor, including being led around the city square riding on the king's own horse, wearing a royal robe that the king had worn, and wearing a crown. The one leading the horse with the honored man riding on it was to proclaim, "Thus it shall be done to the man whom the king desires to honor."

Paraphrase the words of the king (Esther 6:10). ______________________

______________________________________________________________________

After Haman's reluctant display of honor toward Mordecai, Mordecai returned to the king's gate, and Haman went home sulking. And to think, Haman had to do this the morning of Esther's second banquet! What do you think Mordecai was thinking while Haman led him around the town square, saying words of praise? It would almost be a comical scene if it weren't so tragic, wouldn't you say?

Tomorrow we will witness poetic justice at its best!

## Discussion Question

Discuss the words of Mordecai: "For if you remain silent at this time, relief and deliverance will arise from another place." How does the principle that if we are called of God and refuse, He will choose some else to fulfill His purpose apply to us?

## Personal Application Question

Have you ever felt that God had called you to a specific task only to reject His call and then see someone else receive a blessing for his or her obedience? Explain.

Take a few minutes, and write a prayer, asking God to reveal His sovereignty to you in a fresh, new way based on Jeremiah 1:12.

## Day Three

# Poetic Justice

If Mordecai, before whom you have begun to fall, is of Jewish origin,
you will not overcome him, but will surely fall before him.
—Esther 6:13

As Haman recounted to his wife and his friends everything that had happened, his wife and friends apparently suspected that if Mordecai was a Jew, it would mean certain doom for Haman—hence her words in Esther 6:13: "If Mordecai, before whom you have begun to fall, is of Jewish origin, you will not overcome him, but will surely fall before him." While Haman's wife was still speaking these words of dire straits to Haman, the king's eunuchs arrived to escort Haman to the banquet.

The situation went from bad to worse for Haman. At the banquet, King Ahasuerus again asked Esther what was her petition—even up to half of his kingdom. What stunning request did she make? (Esther 7:3–4) ____________________________________________

____________________________________________

The king's anger was roused as he demanded, "Who is he, and where is he, who would presume to do this?" Esther pointed at Haman, saying, "A foe and an enemy is this wicked Haman!" In anger, the king stormed out to the palace garden while Haman fell on the couch and begged Esther for his life—to no avail (Esther 7:5–7). The king returned inside, saw Haman on the couch, and exclaimed, "Will he even assault the queen with me in the house?" As soon as the king spoke these words, his servants covered Haman's face.

One of the servants then told the king about the gallows Haman had built the night before on which he would hang Mordecai. What did the king say when he heard this? (Esther 7:9) ______________

______________________________________________________________________________

The king's officials hanged Haman on the gallows that he had prepared for Mordecai, and the king's anger subsided (Esther 7:10). And that is poetic justice at its finest!

Webster's Dictionary defines *poetic justice* as "justice in which good is properly rewarded and evil punished; justice as one might wish it to be." *Irony* is defined as "a combination of circumstances or a result that is the opposite of what is or might be expected or considered appropriate."

## Discussion Question

Discuss your thoughts on poetic justice and irony in the book of Esther.

## Personal Application Question

In the story of Esther, a guilty man built a gallows to hang an innocent man, but guilt was paid for by the guilty one. In the account of Jesus, a guilty man built a cross to hang an innocent man, and guilt was paid for by the innocent one. How does this apply to you?

Take a few minutes to write a prayer based on Psalm 73:24 asking God to guide you with His counsel.

## *Notes*

Day Four

# A New Edict

Write to the Jews as you see fit.
—Esther 8:8

On the same day that Haman was hanged, Esther inherited the house of Haman, the enemy of the Jews. Esther also disclosed to King Ahasuerus that Mordecai was her cousin and guardian. Then what did Esther do? (Esther 8:3) ____________________, ____________________ ________, ________________________, and __________________________

What did the king do? (Esther 8:4) ____________________________________

Esther asked that the original edict to annihilate the Jews be revoked, but since the king could not recant the previous decree, there was no reason why a counter decree could not be issued. And the king said, "Write to the Jews as you see fit."(Esther 8:8) So with the king's approval, Esther and Mordecai wrote a new decree permitting the Jews to defend themselves and to kill their attackers effective the same day Haman's decree was to have become effective.

When that day arrived, Israel defeated the enemies, including killing the ten sons of Haman. And so justice—poetic justice—was served!

There are many similarities and differences between the decree Haman issued and the decree God issued. The main similarity between the decree issued by Haman and the decree issued by God is that both edicts decreed death.

Haman issued a decree for death; the reason was simply that the people were Jews. God issued a decree for death; the reason was exclusively because of sin. "The soul who sins will die" (Ezekiel 18:4, NASB). Write Romans 6:23. ______________________________

______________________________

______________________________

A simple comparison of the differences between these two decrees shows that Haman's decree was one that demonstrated *partiality;* God's decree was one that manifested *impartiality.* Haman's decree involved *only* Jews; God's decree was for *all* mankind. Write Romans 3:23. ______________

______________________________

______________________________

Haman issued his decree because he hated the Jews—one Jew in particular, Mordecai. God declared His decree because he hated sin and what it did to the people whom He loved. "There are six things which the Lord hates, yes, seven which are an abomination to Him: haughty eyes, a lying tongue, hands that shed innocent blood, a heart that devises wicked plans, feet that run rapidly to evil, a false witness who utters lies, and one who spreads strife among brothers" (Proverbs 6:16–19).

Neither Haman's decree nor God's decree could be revoked. Haman would not and could not revoke his decree because of his hatred for the Jews; God could not and would not revoke His decree because of His holiness. "And so I will show my greatness and my holiness, and I will make myself known in the sight of many nations. Then they will know that I am the LORD" (Ezekiel 38:23, NIV).

Both decrees brought death to their authors. Haman was hung on a gallows; Jesus, God's Son, was hung on a cross. Haman's death was to no avail. Jesus Christ's death gave life.
Write John 5:21. ______________________________

______________________________

______________________________

Haman's law was amended, thereby providing a way of escape for its intended victims. God's law was fulfilled in Christ Jesus, giving life to its called recipients. "Do not think that I (Jesus) came to abolish the Law or the Prophets; I did not come to abolish, but to fulfill" (Matthew 5:17, NASB). The amended law of Haman's deadly decree gave Jews hope and a reason to celebrate. God's fulfilled law gives all people who believe in God's Son the promise of eternal life and a reason to dance and shout for joy. "Then maidens will dance and be glad, young men and old as well. I will turn their mourning into gladness; I will give them comfort and joy instead of sorrow" (Jeremiah 31:13, NIV).

Esther was instrumental in establishing a feast called the Feast of Purim, commemorating the Jews' deliverance from Haman. This was a two-day celebration and was to be observed by every Jew for all generations. A second letter written by Esther and Mordecai established the appointed time with instructions for the times of fasting and the times of lamentations during Purim (Esther 9:31–32).

Mordecai was promoted second *only* to the king and was great among the Jews, because he sought the good of his people and spoke for the welfare of his whole nation. This is the second time a Jew was promoted to the second-highest office in the land that not his own; the first was Joseph, the eleventh son of Jacob/Israel, when he was second *only* to Pharaoh of Egypt.

## Discussion Question

Discuss all the possible emotions Haman may have harbored against Mordecai, a Jew, and why Haman would seek to destroy all the Jews living in the 127 provinces of Xerxes' kingdom.

## Personal Application Question

If you were in a position to save a nation of people, but saving a nation could cost you your life, could and would you still save a nation? Explain.

Take a few minutes to write a prayer based on Mark 9:23, asking God to give you an abundance of faith to be obedient in all circumstances. Use margins if necessary.

We bid farewell to Queen Esther and continue to admire her for her courage and determination to do what is right.

## Day Five

# Virtue Reigns

Trust in the LORD with all your heart, and do
not lean on your own understanding.
—Proverbs 3:5

Did you ever wonder why God chose the people of Israel to be His chosen people? Why not the Philistines, or the Egyptians, or the Edomites? Deuteronomy 7:7 tells us the reasons He did *not* choose the sons of Israel. "The LORD did not set His love on you (Israel) nor choose you because you were more in number than any of the peoples, for you were the fewest of all peoples." God's sovereign choice of Israel was not based on the *size* of the nation. (Abraham received the promise while still childless, Isaac had one son, and Jacob's immediate family consisted of only seventy people). It stemmed from His love and faithfulness to His covenant purpose for them.

David said in 2 Samuel 7:23–24,

> "And who is like your people Israel--the one nation on earth that God went out to redeem as a people for Himself, and to make a name for Himself, and to perform great and awesome wonders by driving out nations and their gods from before your people, whom You redeemed from Egypt? You have established Your people Israel as Your very own forever, and You, O LORD, have become their God." (NIV)

Ezekiel spoke the words of the Lord to the Jewish exiles in Babylon under Nebuchadnezzar to remind the exiles of the sins that had brought God's judgment on them and to assure them of God's future blessing in keeping with His covenant. Listen to his words found in Ezekiel 20:5–6

> Thus says the Lord God, "On the day when I chose Israel and swore to the descendants of the house of Jacob (Israel) and made Myself known to them in the land of Egypt, when I swore to them, saying, I am the Lord your God; on that day I swore to them to bring them out from the land of Egypt into a land that I had selected for them, flowing with milk and honey, which is the glory of all lands."

Ezekiel 20:8 tells us what evil the people of Israel did. List the four charges mentioned here that the Lord had against them.

1. ______________________________
2. ______________________________
3. ______________________________
4. ______________________________

The Lord God certainly did not choose them for their faithfulness, wouldn't you agree?

Hosea 2:19 says, "And I will betroth you to Me forever; Yes, I will betroth you to Me in righteousness and in justice, in loving kindness, and in compassion." The Hebrew word for loving kindness is *hesed.* This word is used about 250 times in the Old Testament and means loyal, steadfast, or faithful love and stresses the idea of a belonging together. Here it connotes God's faithfulness to His unfaithful people.

List four more charges against the Israelites after the Lord God gave them His commandments and statutes in the wilderness according to Ezekiel 20:13.

1. ______________________________
2. ______________________________
3. ______________________________
4. ______________________________

Jeremiah 1:16 says, "God will pronounce His judgments on the people of Israel concerning all their wickedness; forsaking the Lord, offering sacrifices to other gods, and worshipping the works of their own hands."

And why did God keep on forgiving such a stiff-necked people? The Lord said in Ezekiel 20:9, "But I acted for the sake of My name." The preservation of the people of Israel was for the Lord's name's sake in spite of their repeated rebellion in Egypt, on their journey from Egypt in the wilderness, and even in Canaan. God is faithful even when people are not.

Why do you think God chose you to be His follower? What qualifications or credentials can you and I boast of that God should choose us to be His own people? ______________________________

______________________________________________________________________

Isaiah 64:6 reminds us that before we were in Christ, "All our righteous deeds are like filthy rags." After Christ has atoned for our sins, Matthew 5:16 says, "Let your light shine before men in such a way that they may see your good works, and glorify your Father who is in heaven." Who or what made the difference? ______________________________________________

______________________________________________________________________

What if God did not continually forgive us? Are we any different than the people of Israel? What does 1 John 1:8–9 say? ______________________________________________

______________________________________________________________________

______________________________________________________________________

How often are we to forgive one another? See Matthew 18:21–22. ____________________

______________________________________________; in other words, as often as needed.

Does that mean that the Lord God has rejected Israel? On the contrary. Listen to the words Moses said on his 120th birthday as he spoke to the people of Israel in Deuteronomy 31:6: "Be strong and courageous, do not be afraid or tremble at them (enemy), for the Lord your God is the One who goes with you. He will not fail you or forsake you" (NASB). And again in Deuteronomy 31:8, Moses encouraged Joshua as he was about to lead the people of Israel into the Promised Land: "And the Lord is the One who goes ahead of you; He will be with you. He will not fail you or forsake you. Do not fear, or be dismayed" (NASB).

The author of Hebrews quoted Deuteronomy 31:5 to his readers of the New Testament. That is written for our benefit so that we may know that God is faithful for His Name's sake and that we who believe in the name of the Son of God, may know that we have eternal life (1 John 5:13, NASB). "And this is eternal life that we may know the only true God and Jesus Christ whom He has sent" (John 17:3, NASB).

As judge over Israel, Deborah certainly knew the faithfulness of God and obeyed His words. In faith, she looked to God for deliverance for her people. She was filled with courage and acted upon His leading and direction. She drew from knowledge of repeated past sins of her people and God's continual faithfulness to forgive and rescue them time and time again.

Today, mankind is still rebelling against God continually. Yet should we not learn from ancient history and long-ago peoples that God is the same yesterday, today, and forever and is faithful to forgive us our sins for His name's sake, not by works of righteousness that we have done? "But when the kindness of God our Savior and His love for mankind appeared, He saved us, not on the basis of deeds which we have done in righteousness, but according to His mercy" (Titus 3:4–5, NASB).

When Esther went from captive orphan girl to queen over a foreign nation, what do you think went through her mind?____________________________________________________________

________________________________________________________________________________

Esther, like Deborah, was placed in a position to rescue her people. Esther also had to have faith and courage to undertake a seemingly impossible task. Her training in obedience through her older cousin, Mordecai, prepared her to be obedient in a most courageous way when called upon to intercede for her people, who were in a very precarious and deadly situation. Her story gives us hope and encouragement that no matter how deep or where our roots have grown, our flower can bloom in God's Son-light.

You and I, unlike Esther and Deborah, will probably never be called upon to rescue a nation. It amazes me that God would call a woman to do such a heroic task, but then, God did not rely on the strength of these women; they had to rely on His strength, might, and wisdom. However, you and I are called to tasks that are specific to us and our situations—not specific tasks, but tasks that are specific to us. Do you see the difference?

## Discussion Question

Of the eight women we studied—Eve, Sarah, Rebekah, Rachel, Miriam, Deborah, Tamar, and Esther—which one did you most readily identify with and why?

## Personal Application Question

If someone were to write your life story, would there be a testimony to your faith in Jesus Christ and His unfailing faithfulness to you? Explain.

Take a few minutes to write a prayer based on Romans 12:2, asking that the Lord would transform you through the renewal of your mind so that you may understand the good, acceptable, and perfect will of the Lord.

Dear Friend,

When we are obedient to the Lord God as He calls us to "fear the Lord your God, to walk in all His ways, to love Him, and to serve the Lord your God with all your heart and with all your soul" (Deuteronomy 10:12), then, my beloved, we have become women of virtue. Let your light shine that others may see your good works and glorify your Father who is in heaven! (Matthew 5:15)

What a joy this journey has been! Thank you for all your hard work in preparing for each lesson and for your participation in the discussion questions and personal application questions. I give all the glory to our great God for this opportunity to study His Word together. I trust you have grown in your faith in the one true God and Savior, Jesus Christ, as we journeyed together these past eight weeks.

"The Lord bless you and keep you; the Lord make His face to shine upon you, and be gracious to you; the Lord lift up His countenance on you, and give you peace." (Numbers 6:24-26)

*Rita Kroon*

Who can find a virtuous woman? For her price is far above rubies.

# About the Author

Rita Kroon has written

Letters from the Past (biblical historical fiction), You Have Cancer: A Journey through the Valley of the Shadow of Death (the story of her personal journey of faith on the battlefield with cancer), Praying the Scriptures (collection of prayers based on Scripture), children's stories, devotionals, wildlife magazine articles, her own weekly column for area newspaper, poetry, and book reviews.

Rita was first drawn to writing while in high school and believes that in order to be considered a successful Christian author, her writing must first honor the Lord Jesus Christ, and secondly, draw others into a deeper walk of faith with Him through the study of the Scriptures.

She received her associate degree in speech and communications, has attended writers' conferences and participated in creative writing classes, and was an active member in writers' critique groups. Rita is a former member of the Minnesota Christian Writers' Guild

Rita and her husband, Burt, reside in Shoreview, Minnesota and attend Bethlehem Baptist Church in Mounds View, where John Piper pastors. Over the past several years, Rita has been involved in women's ministries, attending and leading women's Bible studies. Rita also works with ESL (English as a Second Language) individuals at their church. Burt is active in the evangelism ministry at Bethlehem Baptist. They have three married daughters and seventeen grandchildren. They are actively involved in each grandchild's life and count each one a blessing.

CPSIA information can be obtained at www.ICGtesting.com
Printed in the USA
BVOW050857231112

306246BV00003B/3/P

9 781462 722563

A woman's beautiful character is determined by her spiritual life. The key to becoming a godly woman is fear of the Lord. A reverence for God is expressed in the submission to His will and is the beginning of knowledge. "A woman who fears the Lord, she shall be praised" (Proverbs 31:30). She lives her faith. She is a beautiful woman of God. She has become a woman of virtue.

An Eight-Week, Condensed Interactive Bible Study for the Woman on the Go

Also by Rita Kroon:

*Letters from the Past*

*You Have Cancer: A Journey through the Valley of the Shadow of Death*

*Praying the Scriptures*

# WOMANHOOD: BECOMING A WOMAN OF VIRTUE

An Eight-Week, Condensed Bible Study

Rita Kroon

The Essence of a Woman Fashions
the Person She Will Become

CROSSBOOKS
PUBLISHING

*CrossBooks™*
*A Division of LifeWay*
*1663 Liberty Drive*
*Bloomington, IN 47403*
*www.crossbooks.com*
*Phone: 1-866-879-0502*



*First published by CrossBooks 11/05/2012*

*ISBN: 978-1-4627-2256-3 (sc)*
*ISBN: 978-1-4627-2255-6 (e)*

*Library of Congress Control Number: 2012920325*



*Printed in the United States of America*

*This book is printed on acid-free paper.*

For my daughters,
LaDawn, René, and Shelly.
For Carol Patterson,
Mary Delk,
and
all the ladies in Bible study.

***What a joy to share***
***the Scriptures with***
***each of you!***

# Table of Contents

# Womanhood
# Becoming a Woman of Virtue

A woman who fears the Lord, she shall be praised
—Proverbs 31:30

## About the Study

The *condensed* Bible study is geared for the woman on the go and is suitable for either an individual study or for a group setting.

Whether you choose the individual or the group option, I am delighted that you and I have this opportunity to discover the treasures that God has in store for us through the study of women of Old Testament times. On the eight-week journey, we will meet the first woman of Eden, dine with the queen of Persia, and meet several women in between.

As we embark on this expedition through the annals of history, we will discover that it is here that the basic lessons of cause and effect, choices and consequences, and obedience and blessing begin their consistent journey down through the centuries.

The women we will meet are, for the most part, ordinary beings. They would not make headlines in any other history book but God's, because there are no unimportant people in God's sight. The fact that God recorded their stories for our learning reveals what He considers important.

Some of the choices and decisions these women face will replay themselves again and again in the history of humanity. As we get to know these women, their choices will challenge us, their faith

will inspire us, their hardships will encourage us, and the lessons they learned will reflect a ready application for our own lives.

As we complete each week's assignments, we will come to know what the Lord is saying to each of us personally as we use the observation-interpretation-application method of study.

*Observation* asks questions about the basic facts—who, what, when, where, and how.

*Interpretation* asks questions that delve into the meaning of the passage of Scripture.

*Application* asks questions that will help us to discover the implication for our own personal growth in Christ Jesus.

We will seek the wisdom of the Holy Spirit as we compare Scripture with Scripture, make use of footnotes, and look at different commentaries; then we will apply to our lives what we have read and understood to be the revealed Word of God.

Each week's study lesson is devoted to one woman of the Old Testament and explores the background, culture, circumstance, and struggles of these eight women with lessons that are relevant to today's woman.

## Individual Condensed Study for the woman on the go

Work at your own pace as you study one woman of the Old Testament per week – approximately one hour per week is typical.

## Group Condensed Study for the women on the go

Participants will meet together once a week for a two-hour session with (ideally) six to seven women per small group. The class members will work together on completing the weekly assignments and discussion questions. There is no homework.

# Introduction

The idea for this particular Bible study, *Womanhood: Becoming a Woman of Virtue,* was first relayed to me by my very dear friend and Bible study leader, Carol Patterson. She read the first two chapters of my book, *Letters from the Past,* and called me, saying, "Girlfriend, you have got to make this into a Bible study!"

The idea began to take a more definite shape when Mary Delk, Director of Women's Ministries at Bethlehem Baptist Church in Minneapolis, Minnesota, suggested that I write a women's Bible study. This was affirmed by the women in the study I was leading at the time.

As I researched and compared Scripture with Scripture, the first chapters began to emerge, and I realized that if I was to be a successful Christian author, my work must first and foremost bring honor to the Lord Jesus Christ; secondly, it must draw others into a deeper walk of faith with Him through the study of His Word. I am reminded of the words of my pastor, John Piper, who said, "God is most glorified when we are most satisfied in Him." To honor the Lord and to be satisfied in Him was, and remains, my motivation to write this Bible study. I pray you also will "Do your best to present yourself to God as one approved, a workman who does not need to be ashamed and who correctly handles the word of truth." (2 Timothy 2:15)

I am delighted you have chosen to put on your sandals, pack your satchels, and journey with me through time and distance to meet and get to know eight women of the Old Testament so that we may apply to our lives the invaluable lessons we glean from each of them.

With God's Word as our map and the Holy Spirit as our guide, let's begin our quest of finding the treasures God has placed before us as we travel from history to the present and from faceless portraits to reflections of our selves.

Welcome to the beginning of time!

*Rita Kroon*

# Eve

Therefore, just as sin entered the world through one man, and death through sin,
and in this way death came to all men, because all have sinned.
—Romans 5:12 (NIV)

The opening statement of the Old Testament in Genesis 1:1 and says, "In the beginning God created the heavens and the earth." The word *beginning* is the natural meaning of the word with reference to time—when time was introduced from the preexisting timelessness of antiquity. "In the beginning"—not of eternity, but of the creation of the world—marks the interruption of the past endless eternity. Time is introduced at the beginning of creation.[1]

The writer of the gospel of John also started his letter with what three words? ________________ ______________________________ However, John used this phrase to mean *eternity.* He wrote in John 1:1–3, "In the beginning was the Word, and the Word was with God, and the Word was God." *In the beginning* here refers to "before time began or timeless existence; continually existing prior to creation; prior to time."[2] Verse 2 says, "He was in the beginning with God." The word *was* actually means "already in existence" or "eternal." Verse 3 records the words, "All things came into being by Him and apart from Him nothing came into being that has come into being."

The one who was in existence from eternity prior to the creation of the world is He whom John described as the one that he and the disciples had seen, heard, and touched. The Word of Life was with the Father in eternity and was manifested to man—not at the creation of the earth but two thousand years ago when the Son of God was born in Bethlehem. "And the Word was made flesh" (John 1:14). God became man! Jesus was the Son of God and Son of Man.

In the beginning, God created the heavens and the earth. The Hebrew word *bara* means "to do or to make" and is used in Genesis 1:25 and also to describe the entire creative activity in Exodus 20:11. Genesis 2:7 uses the word *yatsar* and means "formed." God formed man from the dust of the ground.

According to Genesis 1:3–27, on day one, God created the light and the darkness—day and night. On day two, God made the expanse and separated the waters from below and from above the expanse and called it heaven. On day three, God created the earth and seas—vegetation, plants, and fruit trees. On day four, God created the lights in the expanse of the heavens—the sun, moon, and stars. On day five, God created all species of sea life and birds of the air. On day six, God said, "Let the earth bring forth every living creature; cattle and creeping things and beasts after their kind."

Then God said, "Let us make man in Our image, according to Our likeness to rule over all the earth." (Genesis 1:26) *Us* and *Our* are plurals of majesty. *Image* means "likeness." Man was created in a natural and moral likeness of God. It is when man sinned that he lost the moral likeness, which was his sinlessness.

Mankind was distinct from animals, because man was made in the image of God (Genesis 1:26). Man was to rule over the animals, birds, and sea creatures (Genesis 1:27). Man was formed of the dust of the ground. God breathed *(napah)* the breath of life into man, and man became *(hayah)* a living being (Genesis 2:7).

The Hebrew word *yatsar* means "formed" and gives the picture of a potter at work, forming and molding with his hands the material he holds—in man's case, the dust of the earth. What additional care did God use when He fashioned woman? (Genesis 2:21–22) ____________________

____________________________________________________________

____________________________________________________________

Can you picture the tender scene when God first brought woman to man and presented her to him as his wife? Try to imagine the delight God must have felt to see His creation, beautiful and in perfect harmony. No wonder the Scriptures say, "And God saw that it was good. Very good!" And Adam called her woman, "because she was taken out of man" (Genesis 2:23). Adam also named her Eve, "because she was the mother of all the living" (Genesis 3:20).

God planted every tree that was pleasing to look at and good for food. What two trees of special significance did God plant in the midst of the garden? (Genesis 2:9) ____________________
and ____________________________________________________________

What was God's explicit command to Adam and Eve regarding the tree of knowledge of good and evil? (Genesis 2:16–17)________________________________________

What would be the consequences if Adam and Eve ate of that tree? ____________________

Trouble came to the Garden of Eden when Satan arrived on the scene. In his *original* state, Satan "had the seal of perfection, full of wisdom and perfect in beauty" (Ezekiel 28:12). Satan was the consummation of perfection in his original wisdom and beauty and "on the day Satan was created, all the precious stones were prepared" (Ezekiel 28:13).

But Satan became conceited (1 Timothy 3:6). He became prideful, wanting to raise his throne above the stars of God. His goal was to make himself like the Most High (Isaiah 14:13–14). In Hebrew, the name for God Most High is *El Elyon,* emphasizing God's strength and sovereignty. Satan wanted to rule! Therefore, there was war in heaven, and Satan, the deceiver, and his angels were hurled to the earth (Revelation 12:9).

Satan is introduced in Genesis 3:1 as the serpent and is described as "craftier than any beast of the field which the Lord God had made." The serpent that Satan used was apparently a beautiful creature in its uncursed state. Whether Satan took the form of a serpent or actually possessed the serpent is not clear. *Crafty* means "clever," but not in a degrading sense at this point. And because Satan was crafty, he came in the disguise of whatever suited his purpose.

Let's listen in on the conversation recorded in Genesis 3:1 that Satan initiated with Eve. "Indeed, has God said, 'You shall not eat from any tree of the garden'?" Eve replied, "From the fruit of the trees of the garden we may eat; but from the fruit of the tree which is in the middle of the garden, God has said, 'You shall not eat from it, or touch it, lest you die.'"

Satan did not call out, "Come, I'll teach you to sin!" Satan is much more subtle. He went on to say, "You surely shall not die." *We can almost see Satan slither in for the kill as he boldly contradicted God here.* "For God knows that in the day you eat from it your eyes will be opened and you will be like God, knowing good and evil." *Be **like** God?* The crafty one tried to usurp God's authority. Satan took it upon himself to explain God's purpose in forbidding them to eat from that one tree.

Eve looked at the tree (temptation), saw that it was good for food (lust of the flesh) and a delight to look at (lust of the eyes) and was able to make one wise (pride of life), and she took from its fruit ("Do not even touch the tree") and ate! ("You shall not eat of it.") When someone yields to temptation, *sin* is the result. Then she took from its fruit and gave it to her husband, and he ate. Read 1 Timothy 2:14. Eve was deceived; Adam ate knowingly. Satan's mission: *accomplished!*

Their sin was more than eating forbidden fruit; it was [1]disobeying the revealed word of God, [2]believing the lie of Satan, and [3]placing their own wills above God's. Sin, with all its dreadful consequences, now entered the human race and the world in general. (Genesis 3:6) Read Romans 5:12.

The same three areas of Eve's self-deception are in the same categories of *temptation* as those found in 1 John 2:16—the lust of the flesh, the lust of the eyes, and the pride of life.
We are all prone to sin. Write Romans 3:10. ______________________________

______________________________________________________________

Running from God with no place to hide is a scary place to be, wouldn't you agree? This is especially true when guilt, shame, and fear are chasing in hot pursuit. But that is what Adam and Eve tried to do—run from God with no place to hide. See Genesis 3:8. When the Lord God asked, "Where are you?" the man explained that he was naked and afraid; therefore, he hid himself. Adam experienced guilt, shame, and fear because of his sin.

When the Lord God questioned Adam further regarding his nakedness and whether or not he had eaten from the tree that God commanded him not to eat from, the man actually blamed God for his sin. Genesis 3:12 says: "The woman whom Thou gavest to be with me, she gave me from the tree, and I ate." Then Lord then asked Eve her side of the story, and she replied, "The serpent deceived me, and I ate." The Lord God did not give Satan a chance to confess his sin, because there would be no forgiveness for him; rather, the Lord put a curse on him, saying, "Because you have done this, cursed are you more than all cattle ... I will put enmity between you and the woman, and between your seed (spiritual descendants of Satan) and her seed (those who are in the family of God); He (namely, Christ) shall bruise you on the head (will deal a death blow to Satan's head) and you shall bruise Him on the heel" (cause Him to suffer). (Genesis 3:14–15)

How God must have grieved in His heart! How His indignation and wrath must have been set ablaze! But in spite of sin, His unconditional love never wavered; His righteousness was never compromised.

> As the echo of the crunching of the fruit was still in the garden, Jesus was leaving for Calvary.[3]

God's unimaginable plan was unfathomable in its scope, unprecedented in its purpose, unmatched in its wisdom, and unstoppable in its accomplishment! What great news!

Many people will try to blame others—even God—for their sin, but "each one of us shall give account of himself to God" (Romans 14:12). Others will try to justify themselves by putting their faith and confidence in a pastor or priest, their own good works, their church, their family background, their ability to keep the Ten Commandments, their knowledge of God, or a host of other means to try

to gain salvation, but it will be to no avail. "There is no one righteous, not even one; all have turned away, they have together become worthless; there is no one who does good, not even one" (Romans 3:10, 12, NIV).

Sin entered the world, and each one of us is born into sin and cannot enter the presence of a holy God with sin. Listen to the heart of the gospel found in 2 Corinthians 5:21. "He made Him who knew no sin to be sin on our behalf that we might become the righteousness of God in Him." How awesome that "God demonstrated His own love toward us, in that while we were yet sinners, Christ died for us" (Romans 5:8). We can trust in the words of John 1:12: "But as many as received Him, who believed in His name, He gave the right to become children of God."

Genesis 3:21 says that the Lord God made garments to cover the nakedness of Adam and Eve. What do you think is the significance of this act?________________________________________

________________________________________________________________

(Keep in mind the fact that when the first couple sinned, the first thing they realized was that they were naked, and they tried to hide.)

## Discussion Question

What are some far-reaching consequences of our choices—either through our own self-deception (things we reason as justifiable to sway our decision to yield to temptation) or through the lies of the deceiver? Are the consequences the same? Explain.

## Personal Application Question

How do you personally "submit therefore to God. Resist the devil and he will flee from you"? (James 4:7)

## PRAYER:

"Instruct us in the fear of you, O Lord, to hate evil, pride and arrogance and the evil way (Proverbs 8:13). Teach us to be strong against temptation and to be tender toward doing good." Add your own words of prayer.

We bid farewell to Eve, as she and her husband were banished from the beautiful garden. She was cursed to suffer pain in childbirth and to be subject to her husband. Punishment was pronounced on Adam; he would have to earn a living by the sweat of his brow. The ground was destined to grow weeds, and Satan was made to crawl on his belly and eat dust. But God, in His infinite love, grace, and mercy, did not abandon our first couple. He provided garments for them as a sign of His grace and mercy, and He made a promise that forgiveness of sins would be made in and through His Son.

[1]Kapp, Jacob W. *Beginning,* (Chicago, Illinois: International Standard Bible Encyclopedia, edited by James Orr, 1915)
[2] Ibid.
[3]Lucado, Max. *And the Angels were Silent* (Sisters, Oregon: Multnomah Publishers, 1992), 25.
[4]Kroon, Rita. *Praying the Scriptures* (Denver, Colorado: Outskirts Press, 2011), 64.

# Sarah

From of old no one has heard or perceived by the ear, no eye has
seen a God besides you, who acts for those who wait for Him.
—Isaiah 64:4 (ESV)

After Adam and Eve were banished from their garden home and the angel with the flaming sword stood guard at the entrance, the Garden of Eden, which at one time captivated the essence of God's created beauty, became uninhabited and overgrown with weeds. It became symbolic of man's depraved and sinful condition.

Today, we will start our journey through distance and time from the Garden of Eden to a land more spacious and fertile than it was beautiful and lush. We are going to Canaan to visit with Sarah, Abraham's wife. Before we proceed, however, let's look over our shoulders to see their background.

Ten generations after the flood, Abram was born from the descendants of Shem, one of Noah's three sons, in 2165 BC. Abram's name means "exalted father"—the progenitor of God's chosen people, who were first called Hebrews. Two generations later, they were called the people of Israel, and then they became known as Jews. Later, Abram's name was changed to Abraham. Abraham was married to the woman we plan to spend time with this week. Originally, her name was Sarai, but it was later changed to Sarah. For the remainder of this week's study, we will refer to Abram and Sarai as Abraham and Sarah.

Early in their marriage, Abraham and Sarah lived with Abraham's father, Terah, and Abraham's nephew, Lot, in Ur among the Chaldeans. Now the Chaldeans were a wealthy, sophisticated, and

pagan people. According to Joshua 26:2, Abraham's father, Terah, also served other gods. In other words, he worshipped idols, so we can safely assume that Abraham did likewise.

It was from this background and culture and after the death of Abraham's father that God called Abraham to take Sarah, his nephew, the servants, and all their flocks and herds and come out from among this people to a land that God would show him—a rich and fertile land called Canaan. Notice that *God called Abraham;* Abraham did not seek the Lord.

Let's take a look at Abraham's qualifications. Why should he be called by God to be the one from whom God would make a great nation—a nation with people too numerous to count; a nation with a king who was said to have a heart after God's own heart; a nation from which the Savior of the *world* would come?

So far, we have seen that Abraham's father was an idol worshipper. Abraham also served other gods, lived among a pagan people, was a nomad, was rich, and was married to Sarah, who was barren. There were no outstanding godly qualifications in this man, wouldn't you agree?

For a clue as to why God called Abraham, we have to go back to the days immediately after the flood. God spoke to Noah, as recorded in Genesis 9:11: "And I will establish My covenant with you." Noah spoke a blessing on one of his sons, Shem, saying, "Blessed be the Lord, the God of Shem" (Genesis 9:26). God (Yahweh) would be Shem's God and blessing. (Jews are of Semitic—"from Shem"—descent.) Recall that Abraham was descended from Shem. God chose the Jews to be His chosen people through whom He would call *all* nations to Himself.

Let's look at Sarah's qualifications that she should be the mother of this great nation. Sarah was a Hebrew maiden of remarkable beauty with dark luminous eyes and dark hair. Surely she was not one to go unnoticed. She must have captured the admiration of the Chaldean shepherds, wouldn't you agree? Sarah also had a quiet strength and graceful dignity. She had a submissive spirit which became evident when she agreed to pick up and move, *without complaint,* to a far-away country. Don't miss that rare quality. Do you think one's beauty or submissive spirit qualifies one to be called of God for such an amazing role in God's plan and purpose? ______________________
Explain.______________________________________________

______________________________________________

______________________________________________

Think about your own qualifications. Which of your characteristics might make you worthy to be called by God? ______________________________________________
I couldn't think of a single qualification, either, that would entitle me to be called by God—*apart from Jesus Christ,* that is.

What about Jesus? Let's look at His credentials. Read Hebrews 1:2–4, and list nine attributes that describe Jesus that cannot be said of man.

1. ______________________________
2. ______________________________
3. ______________________________
4. ______________________________
5. ______________________________
6. ______________________________
7. ______________________________
8. ______________________________
9. ______________________________

Jesus is the "radiance of His (God's) glory," (Hebrews 1:3) meaning effulgence or flood of resplendent light. The word means an outshining; not a reflection. We are to reflect God's glory; Jesus **is** God's glory!

Abraham may not have had impressive qualifications, but he had a heart to believe and a mind to obey and in God's eyes, it was counted as righteousness. We see his faith in action when he obeyed the Lord when called to go to Canaan. Rather than cross the Arabian Desert, Abraham took Sarah and his nephew Lot and all their possessions and followed the Euphrates River to Haran, in Syria, and then traveled down to Canaan. How old was Abraham when they set out for Canaan? (Genesis 12:4) ______________________________ Sarah was sixty-five!

While in route to Canaan, the Lord appeared again to Abraham, declaring that He would give all this land to his *descendants*. When Abraham told Sarah that the Lord would bless him and make his descendants as numerous as the dust of the earth, do you suppose Sarah had the faintest curiosity as to how this was going to happen? After all, she had never borne any children to Abraham and was well beyond childbearing years. Sarah had little hope of ever conceiving a child! But what does Genesis 15:6 say about Abraham? ______________________________

______________________________

Ten years had passed from the time the Lord had made a covenant with Abraham to bless him with descendants as numerous as the dust of the earth or as numerous as the stars in the heavens—and still no children. Sarah became impatient and was desperate to have children. And Sarah had a plan!

Sarah would give her Egyptian maidservant to Abraham to bear children! What was her maid's name? (Genesis 16:1) ______________________ (Hagar was one of several servants given to Abraham and Sarah while they took refuge in Egypt, where they detoured from a severe famine while in route

to Canaan.) Giving her maidservant to Abraham was a desperate measure to the core, wouldn't you say? But then, we usually are desperate when we try to tip the hand of God in our favor. Abraham must have been torn between believing that he would have descendants and watching his wife suffer the anguish of not having children. What did Abraham do? See Genesis 16:2. ________________

________________________________________________________________

We can all think of times when we ran ahead of the Lord, trying to make His plans come to fruition on *our* timetable and not waiting for the Lord to bring it to pass, can we not? See Isaiah 64:4. Do these plans of *ours* usually meet with success and blessing or disaster and disappointment?

When Hagar saw that she had conceived, how did she feel toward her mistress, Sarah? See Genesis 16:4. ________________________________________________________________
How did Sarah treat Hagar? (Genesis 16:6) ________________________________ There was so much contention between Sarah and Hagar that Hagar fled. However, the angel of the Lord found Hagar in the wilderness, comforted her, and then told Hagar to return to Sarah.

How old was Abraham when Hagar bore a son to him? (Genesis 16:16) ________________
What did Abraham name his son? (Genesis 16:15) ________________ (Arabs are descendants of Ishmael; therefore, many Arabs consider Abraham their forefather and thus Palestine as their land.) (Genesis 17:20) However, Ishmael was not the son from whom the Lord would bless Abraham.

After the birth of Ishmael and for several years thereafter, the tension, anger, bitterness, and resentment between Sarah and Hagar mounted to the breaking point. Hagar fled once again, taking her son with her! Again, the angel of the Lord found Hagar and her son, who was dying of thirst, in the wilderness. He provided them with water and then told Hagar to return to her mistress.

Perhaps you have a friend or a family member with whom you have unsettled contention, anger, bitterness, or resentment. Maybe this elephant in the room shows up silently at family gatherings year after year. Maybe all those phone calls to share something exciting or pressing with that special friend have stopped. What if the person who is presently alienated from you called and asked for forgiveness? What would you do? ________________________________________

________________________________________________________________

________________________________________________________________

What if *you* were the one to make that phone call or personal visit? How do you think the other person would react? ________________________________________________

________________________________________________________________

________________________________________________________________

________________________________________________________________

Write Ephesians 4:31–32. ______________________________________________

______________________________________________________________

______________________________________________________________

______________________________________________________________

______________________________________________________________

______________________________________________________________

One day, when Abraham was ninety-nine years old and Sarah was eighty-nine, as they stayed in the shade of their tent, three men approached along the dusty road. Abraham went out to greet them; Sarah remained in the tent. As the men conversed, one of them said, "I will surely return to you at this time next year, and behold, Sarah your wife shall have a son" (Genesis 18:10). The promise may have been made to Abraham, but it most definitely was meant for Sarah's ears as well, wouldn't you say?

In the privacy of her tent, Sarah did what you and I would probably have done if we were in her sandals. She laughed to herself. The absurdity of such a statement—that she should have a son! She was eighty-nine years old and would be ninety when her son would be born if it were true! How ludicrous! How preposterous!

But then Sarah heard the man say, "Is anything too difficult for the LORD?" (Genesis 18:14) When she heard those words, a trickle of hope began to infiltrate her soul, much like melting snow of early spring drips off a roof and seeps into the soil. Think of a time when you had lost all expectation in a particular situation but then you got a glimmer of hope. Was your faith renewed? Explain. _______

______________________________________________________________

______________________________________________________________

______________________________________________________________

______________________________________________________________

What did Sarah, as well as each of us, need to know about the Lord? See Genesis 18:14, Psalm 86:5, Proverbs 3:5–6, and Matthew 19:26. ________________________________________

______________________________________________________________

______________________________________________________________

At the appointed time the following year, the Lord did for Sarah as He had promised, and Sarah did indeed conceive and have a son (Genesis 21:1–2). They named him Isaac, which means "he laughs" or "laughter." Sarah, of course, was overjoyed! "Who would have said to Abraham that Sarah would nurse children? Yet I have borne him a son in his old age!" Sarah said (Genesis 21:7). It is with her joy in our hearts that we say goodbye to Sarah and Abraham and their cherished son, Isaac, as we travel on to meet Rebekah.

## Discussion Question

Discuss the difference between the *temptation* of Eve and the *trial* of Sarah. What is the end result if we do not resist temptation? ____________________
What does James 1:2–3 say regarding trials? Temptation is of Satan for our destruction; trials are of God for our perfection. See James 1:13–14.

## Personal Application Question

When waiting for answered prayer seems endless, what action(s) are you mostly likely to take?

| | |
|---|---|
| ______ Pray for patience | ______ Call a friend |
| ______ Take control | ______ Become discouraged |
| ______ Give up | ______ Lose faith |
| ______ Become angry | ______ Wait quietly |
| ______ Keep on keeping on | ______ Other |

Take a few minutes, and write a prayer based on Psalm 27:14.

# Rebekah

They have taught their tongues to lie; they weary themselves with sinning.
—Jeremiah 9:5 (NIV)

We bid a joyful farewell to Sarah in Hebron in the land of Canaan, but before take our leave of our elderly friend entirely, let's see what happened with their beloved son, Isaac.

God tested Abraham in a most unusual way. What did God tell Abraham to do? (Genesis 22:2)________________________________________

God does not tempt anyone with evil, as James pointed out in James 1:13. To tempt is to test, try, prove, or solicit to evil. James 1:2 says, "Consider it all joy, my brethren, when you encounter various trials," and James 1:12 says, "Blessed is the man who remains steadfast under trial, for when he has stood the test he will receive the crown of life, which God has promised to those who love him." The same Greek word is used to mean trials that are designed to prove the quality of one's character. We can be confident that God was t__s__i__g Abraham and not t__m__t__n__ him. We never have to fear being tempted (to solicit to evil) by God. We can be certain that all temptations come from either Satan or ourselves. See James 1:14.

When Isaac asked Abraham where was the lamb for the sacrifice, Abraham answered, "God will provide for Himself the lamb." Indeed, God did provide the sacrifice—a ram caught in a thicket. Read Ephesians 5:2, 1 John 2:2, and 1 John 4:10. Who was the ultimate sacrifice? ____________

Have you ever felt that God tested you to the outer limits of your faith? Explain. ____________

________________________________________________

________________________________________________

Is evidence of your faith enough to be an *encouragement* or a *detriment* to others? ______________

________________________________________________

When Isaac reached manhood and Abraham was well advanced in years, Abraham had one more mission to accomplish—to find a wife for Isaac. So he sent his trusted servant to his own relatives in Mesopotamia to find a wife suitable for Isaac. Sarah, however, did not live to meet her daughter-in-law but died with the confidence that God would bless Isaac with descendants too numerous to number.

When the camel caravan of Abraham's servant arrived at its destination, the servant prayed a very specific request. "O Lord, the God of my master Abraham, please grant me success today … I am standing by the spring, and the daughters of the men of the city are coming out to draw water; now may it be that the girl to whom I say, 'Please let down your jar so that I may drink,' and who answers, 'Drink, and I will water your camels also'; may she be the one whom You have appointed for Your servant Isaac" (Genesis 24:14). When was his prayer answered? (Genesis 24:15) ______________

________________________________________________

How was Rebekah described in Genesis 24:16?________________________________

Rebekah's family consented to the marriage arrangement, but most importantly, Rebekah agreed. "I will go," she said (Genesis 24:58). Rebekah's family sent her, along with her maids, on their way with these words found in Genesis 24:60: "May you, our sister, become thousands of ten thousands, and may your descendants possess the gate of those who hate them" (have victory over their enemies).

It was almost evening when Isaac went out to meditate in the quietness and solitude of the field. As he walked along, perhaps he was speculating whether the servant had success in finding his perfect match. Maybe he was contemplating the death of his mother and feeling the loss of not having his mother there to meet his bride. Maybe he was anticipating the soon return of the servant and was eager to see what kind of woman would have such confidence and determination that she would travel over five hundred miles to marry a man she had never met. As he walked along a furrow, he looked up and saw a caravan of camels approaching. He quickened his step to meet them.

And Rebekah lifted up her eyes and saw a man in the field coming towards them. When she saw the man, she dismounted from her camel and asked the servant, "Who is that man walking in the field to meet us?" The servant answered, "He is my master" (Genesis 24:65). Surely her heart must have beat a little faster when she realized she was about to meet the man she was to marry!

Rebekah behaved herself very becomingly when she met Isaac; understanding who he was, she "alighted off her camel" (Genesis 24:64) and "took a veil, and covered herself" (Genesis 24:65) as a sign of humility, modesty, and subjection.

Read Genesis 24:67. According to Gen. 25:19, Jacob was forty years old when he took Rebekah to be his wife, but Jacob was sixty years old when Rebekah gave birth to twin boys. Prior to the birth of the twins, Rebekah felt a struggle within her womb. She was perplexed about this and inquired of the Lord. Listen to the words of His reply found in Genesis 25:23: "Two nations are in your womb; and two peoples shall be separated from your body; and one people shall be stronger than the other; and the older shall serve the younger." The struggle within Rebekah's womb foreshadowed the struggle between the two peoples (the Edomites and the Israelites) of which Esau and Jacob were the progenitors.

When the boys were born, the first one was red and hairy all over, like he was wearing a garment. Isaac and Rebekah named him Esau. Afterward, his brother was born with his hand holding onto Esau's heel, and they named him Jacob, which means "heel catcher" or "trickster."

When the boys grew up, Esau was a skilled hunter and outdoorsman. Jacob was a peaceful man, amiable, and cultured. Isaac loved Esau, because Isaac had a taste for wild game, but Rebekah loved Jacob.

Did your parents have favorites? Did this partiality add tension to your family dynamics? Explain. _

---

---

James 2:9 says, "But if you show partiality you are committing sin." Acts 10:35 paints a beautiful picture of God's impartiality. Peter said, "I most certainly understand now that God is not one to show partiality, but in every nation the man who fears Him and does what is right, is welcome to Him." God looks at the heart, not the nationality, status, or gender.

One day, when Jacob had cooked stew, Esau came in from the field, and he was famished! Esau asked for a bowl of stew, but Jacob responded, "First sell me your birthright." (The birthright of the eldest son gave him precedence over his brothers, assuring him a double share of his father's inheritance [Deuteronomy 21:17].) The birthright could be forfeited by committing a serious sin, and it could also be bartered. Jacob gave Esau bread and the lentil stew, and Esau ate, drank, rose, and went on his way. The transaction was legally binding, since it was sealed with an oath between the two brothers. Thus Esau despised his birthright (Genesis 25:34).

The author of Hebrews said, "See to it that no one comes short of the grace of God; that no root of bitterness springing up causes trouble, and by it many are defiled; that there be no immoral or godless person like Esau, who sold his own birthright for a single meal. For you know that even afterwards, when he desired to inherit the blessing, he was rejected, for he found no place for repentance, though he sought for it with tears." (Hebrews 12:15–17)

Isaac was a very rich man and continued to grow richer until he became very wealthy (Genesis 26:13). Therefore, to receive his inheritance through the birthright was no small thing. Clearly, Esau was not interested in gaining his father's wealth—only in satisfying his needs at the moment.

Many years passed since that incident, and it was time for Isaac to give the blessing. Isaac was very old and nearly blind. Isaac asked Esau to hunt for his favorite game, prepare a savory dish, and bring it to him, and he would bless Esau. (A blessing is different than the birthright. A *blessing* means the handing over of legal power, which is more valuable than any amount of goods or property given in the *birthright*. The blessing was something that fathers gave to each of their sons. Receiving the blessing meant being the head of the clan and having all the power for making decisions for the entire clan.)

Rebekah overheard the plan (Genesis 27:6) and immediately sent for Jacob. Rebekah came up with a very elaborate plan to deceive Isaac, whereby he would give the blessing to Jacob instead of Esau. Jacob was to go to the flock and bring two choice kids from there, and she would prepare a savory dish for his father. Isaac would surely bless Jacob. Jacob questioned the possibility of his father recognizing him; if recognized, Jacob knew he would be considered a deceiver in Isaac's sight and thereby bring a curse upon himself and not a blessing. But Rebekah said, "Your curse be on me, my son; only obey my voice, and go quickly, get them for me." Jacob agreed and left immediately to go get the kid goats.

Rebekah made the savory stew and bread. Then she took Esau's best garments and put them on Jacob so Jacob would smell like the field. She also took the skins of the kids and put them on Jacob's hands and on the smooth part of his neck. Rebekah gave the stew and the bread to Jacob and sent him in to his father.

As my mother used to say, "O, the tangled web we weave, when first we practice to deceive!"

Have you ever been caught in a web—either by your own choice or because you were made part of the web through someone else's actions? Think about that situation for a moment. Was there any justification for the lies? Did the end justify the means? Were there consequences?

When Isaac asked Jacob, "Who are you?" what did Jacob reply? (Genesis 27:19)________________ __________________ After questioning Jacob further, smelling his clothing, and feeling his hands and neck, even though Isaac was not thoroughly convinced, he blessed Jacob! The blessing—given in legal, irreversible form—guaranteed that Jacob would be the head of the household, with all the legal rights and ramifications that accompanied such a position.

When Esau learned that Jacob had received the blessing, he cried out with an exceedingly great and bitter cry, "Do you have only one blessing, my father?" What did Isaac conclude? (Genesis 27:35) ____________________

____________________

What if you were in Rebekah's sandals at that moment—what do you think you would have felt? ____________________

____________________

Isaac did indeed have a blessing for Esau and his descendants, but not one that meant pleasantness. Rather, they would live in a less fertile land and live by the sword (Genesis 27:39–40).

Consider the consequences of this family's favoritism, deceit, lies, anger, bitterness, grudges, and quarreling. Isaac was grieved to have to give his favorite son a blessing that meant hardship and the sword for Esau and his descendants. Esau bore a hateful grudge against Jacob that festered into a threat to kill him. Jacob had to flee for his life to Rebekah's brother (Laban), and Rebekah never saw her beloved son, Jacob, again. These were severe consequences; would you concur?

God had already chosen Jacob as the one He would bless through the covenant that he had made to Abraham and Isaac, since God knew of Esau's spiritual blindness and rebellious heart while they were still struggling in Rebekah's womb. ("The older shall serve the younger" [Genesis 25:23].) Do you wonder how God might have brought it about? One thing is certain; it would have been far better than the way the Isaacs handled it, wouldn't you agree?

Deception is merely a different form of lying, and what does God's Word say about lying or deceiving? Leviticus 19:11 says, "Do not steal. Do not lie. Do not deceive one another" (NIV). And Jeremiah 9:5 says, "They have taught their tongues to lie; they weary themselves with sinning."

What do you think were Rebekah's motives for lying and deceiving Isaac? Check the one that seems most likely.

_______ She reasoned to herself that Jacob would ensure the survival of the clan, whereas Esau could very likely sell out to someone for whatever present need he may have.
_______ She favored Jacob so much that she could not bear to have Esau receive the blessing.
_______ Rebekah had a better chance of being cared for by Jacob than Esau.
_______ She resented Esau for bartering away his birthright and felt that he did not deserve the blessing.
_______ Other

## Discussion Question

Discuss the challenges of not showing favoritism versus loving the unlovely equally and ways people and families spiral out of control against the backdrop of Psalm 79:9.

## Personal Application Question

Do you struggle with lying, telling half-truths, or being deceitful? What motives do you recognize to be at the core?

Take a few minutes to write a prayer, asking God to help you "do your best to present yourself to God as one approved, a workman who does not need to be ashamed and who correctly handles the word of truth" (2 Timothy 2:15).

Because Rebekah made herself vulnerable to us, we glimpse our own reflection in varying degrees and are reminded that "but for the grace of God, there go I." In next week's lesson, we will track with Jacob as he leads us to the next woman we will meet and spend time with.

# Rachel

Blessed is the man whose sin the LORD does not count
against him and in whose spirit is no deceit.
—Psalm 32:2 (NIV)

Sarah's last concern was for her beloved son, Isaac, and Rebekah's final regard was for her cherished son, Jacob. However, neither woman lived to see the fulfillment of God's covenant made to Abraham and Isaac to bless them with descendants too numerous to count.

Let's rejoin Jacob from last week's lesson as he traveled to his mother's relatives in Mesopotamia. Remember that Jacob fled under Esau's threats to kill him because of his deception. Jacob did not have time to gather belongings or servants but left with only his staff and the clothes on his back.

At last, Jacob arrived at his destination. When Jacob looked up, he spotted a well in the field with three flocks of sheep lying beside it, for from the well, the shepherds watered the flocks. When all the flocks were gathered there, they would roll the large stone from the mouth of the well, water the sheep, and put the stone back in its place.

Genesis 29:4–8 records Jacob's conversation with the shepherds at the well. Jacob said, "My brothers, where are you from?" They answered, "We are from Haran." Jacob said, "Do you know Laban?" They replied, "We know him." Jacob asked, "Is it well with him?" They answered, "It is well, and behold, Rachel his daughter is coming with the sheep."

While they were still speaking, Rachel came with her father's sheep. Jacob wasted no time swinging into action to try to impress Rachel. He went up to the well, singlehandedly rolled the heavy stone

from its mouth, and watered her flock! Assuredly, Jacob noticed that Rachel was beautiful of form and face and had sparkling eyes.

Jacob greeted her appropriately with a kiss and introduced himself as Jacob, Rebekah's son. When Rachel heard that he was a relative, she ran to get her father, Laban, leaving Jacob at the well, tending her father's flock.

Not long thereafter, Laban came running. Laban embraced Jacob and brought him back to his house to live. Jacob settled in, and after a month of working for Laban, Laban asked, "Tell me, what shall your wages be?" When Laban said these words, he actually reduced Jacob to the status of a servant—our first suspicious hint of something amiss.

By this time, of course, Jacob had met Leah, Rachel's older sister, but his heart belonged to Rachel. Since Jacob did not have enough wages to pay the customary price for a bride, Jacob said, "I will serve you seven years for your younger daughter Rachel." Laban agreed (Genesis 29:18). Can you imagine planning your wedding for seven years? It is hard to fathom that the seven years went by quickly, for "they seemed like a few days because of his love for her" (Genesis 29:20).

We have been invited to attend a wedding—a wedding seven years in the making! The long-anticipated day finally arrived! The sheep were shorn; the dark fleece was washed, dried in the sun, combed, and spun into yarn for the tent that Jacob and Rachel would share on their wedding night. The flax was harvested and made into fine linen for her wedding garments. The women prepared the food for the wedding feast; the choicest wine was in place. Laban made the arrangements for the wedding night. All was ready.[1]

After Laban had gathered all the men in the place according to their custom, they feasted the day away. You and I wait with Rachel in unbridled anticipation that evening for her father to come to escort her to the wedding tent. Do not our own hearts soar for their pure love that would be made complete?

But the long hours dragged for Rachel. Evening turned to night. Night turned to dawn, and with the dawn came a nightmare so horrendous and incomprehensible that her words were strangled in her screams of betrayal! Leah emerged from the wedding tent! (Genesis 29:25)

Laban had deceived Jacob. Instead of bringing Jacob his cherished Rachel, Laban brought Leah. We stand with Rachel in stunned silence as the deception and betrayal from her own father and older sister nearly choked the life right out of her.

Lies, betrayal, and deception seemed to linger in this family. We first witnessed this human fault when Jacob deceived Esau out of his birthright. Then Jacob joined ranks with Rebekah when they lied and deceived Isaac into giving the blessing to Jacob. Thereupon, Rebekah had to deceive Isaac once again in order to have Isaac bless Jacob before sending him on his way to prevent Esau from murdering her favorite son, Jacob. Now we see that Rebekah's brother, Laban, Rachel's father, took the reins of deception that were bridled with betrayal as he trampled his youngest daughter's dreams into muddy mire. Why? What was Laban's reasoning for doing such a thing? See Genesis 29:26. __

______________________________________________________________

How did Jacob respond? (Genesis 29:25) ______________________________

Notice the callous proposition Laban made to Jacob in Genesis 29:27. "Complete the week of festivities of this one, and we will give you the other also for the service which you shall serve with me for another seven years." It almost sounds like bartering for sheep, wouldn't you agree? But Jacob served Laban another seven years and was rewarded with Rachel as his bride. He also served Laban for another six years for the flocks and herds.

Leah bore sons to Jacob, but Rachel was barren. What was Leah's motive for having sons? See Genesis 29:32–34. ______________________________________________

It wasn't long before jealousy reared its head. Who became jealous of whom? (Genesis 30:1) ______

______________________________________________________________

Would it be safe to say it was because one sister had Jacob's love and the other sister had his children?

What same desperate tactic did Rachel implement that Sarah had also used with her husband, Abraham? See Genesis 30:3. . After Rachel's maidservant bore Jacob two sons, how did Rachel feel? (Genesis 30:8) ______________________________________________

______________________________ How did Leah retaliate? (Genesis 30:9)

______________________________________________________________

______________________________________________________________

After several years, Jacob had fathered six sons and one daughter with Leah, two sons by Rachel's maid, and two sons with Leah's maid. But Rachel was still barren.

But then God intervened on Rachel's behalf, and she conceived, had a son, and named him Joseph (Genesis 30:24). God once again proved faithful regardless of man's actions.

When Jacob told Rachel and Leah that he wanted to go back to his homeland, the sisters agreed, saying something puzzling. "Are we not reckoned by our father as foreigners? For he had sold us, and has also entirely consumed our purchase price." Did Rachel and Leah surmise that their father had used them to get dependable help for fourteen years from Jacob? Jacob surely must have recognized this. Look what he did (Genesis 31:17–18). Jacob secretly gathered Rachel and Leah, their maidservants, his children, and his flocks and herds and fled. In leaving in this manner, what did Jacob do to Laban? (Genesis 31:20) ____________________
What did Rachel do? (Genesis 31:19) ____________________
____________________

When Laban heard the news, he pursued Jacob and his household for seven days, catching up to them in the hill country. Laban spoke angrily and harshly, saying, "Why did you flee secretly … and did not allow me to kiss my sons and my daughters (grandchildren)? …Why did you steal my gods?" (Genesis 31:27-28, 30)

Jacob was so certain that no one in his household had stolen the gods that he said, "The one with whom you find your gods shall die." Jacob did not know that Rachel had stolen them. Laban searched every tent and lastly, Rachel's tent. But Rachel had hidden the idols in the saddle and sat on them. Laban burst into her tent and began searching in vain. Rachel apologized for not being able to rise before her father, because the "manner of women" was upon her.

The meeting between Jacob and Laban ended in a mutual nonaggressive pact. However, Scripture is silent as to whether Rachel and her father ever resolved the deeply wounding issues that hung like a room-darkening curtain between them. Perhaps you have unsettled issues that linger in the pages of your mind. If you had a spiritual ledger, would your accounts payable be checked as "paid in full," or is there unfinished business left to tend to—forgiveness toward another, anger issues, jealousy, deception, rebellion, unconfessed sin, or seeking forgiveness from another? Why not settle your account ledger now?

While in route to Canaan, Jacob sent messengers to Esau, commanding them to say to Esau that he was returning with many flocks, herds, and servants and that he hoped to find favor with Esau. The messengers reported back that Esau was coming to meet him with four hundred men! (Genesis 32:5–6)

Jacob switched to panic mode! He divided his household into two groups, thinking that if Esau killed one group, the other group may survive. He took Rachel, Leah, their two maids, and his twelve children across the ford of the Jabbok. After Jacob did all he could to ensure the safety of his family, he prayed to God, asking for protection for his family. He reminded God of His command

to return to his country, that the Lord God would prosper him, and that He would be with Jacob wherever he went.

As much as I'd like to stay huddled with Rachel, the other women, and their children, let's go back over the tributary of the Jordan and see how Jacob fared alone in the night.

We find Jacob wrestling with a man for the entire night. We listen quietly as Jacob agonized in prayer, weeping and imploring the man's favor. Suddenly, we hear a cry of pain, and we watch in silence as Jacob continued to wrestle with a dislocated hip. Just before dawn, the man asked Jacob his name. Jacob replied, "Jacob." Then the man said, "Your name shall no longer be Jacob, but Israel," which means "he fights or persists with God in prevailing prayer."

"Therefore, if anyone is in Christ, he is a new creation: the old has gone, the new has come!" (2 Corinthians 5:17, NIV) Jacob became a new man. No longer was he the deceiver. One cannot encounter Jesus Christ and not be affected in some way or other, wouldn't you agree?

After an exhausting and sleepless night, Jacob gathered his family together, and when he looked up, he saw Esau coming—and four hundred men with him. How did Esau receive Jacob? (Genesis 33:4)

______________________________________________

Was there complete forgiveness and restoration of their relationship? ____________________

God told Jacob to take his family and go to Bethel, where God had confirmed the Abrahamic covenant to Jacob, and to live there. Therefore, Jacob called for his entire household to put away the foreign gods, purify themselves, change their garments, and rid themselves of any heathen practices. Rachel gladly gave up the idols she had stolen from her father and joined Jacob in worship of the true God. Explain the dynamics that may have transpired between Jacob and Rachel at that moment. _

______________________________________________

______________________________________________

While still in route, Rachel went into very severe labor. With Jacob at her side, Rachel's cries of pain were silenced forever just after giving birth. We grieve with Jacob at the death of his deeply-loved wife. Jacob found comfort in the birth of his son, whom he named Benjamin. His sons became known as the twelve tribes (sons) of Israel. Levi became the priestly tribe; Moses, Aaron, and Miriam were from this tribe. Judah was the kingly tribe from which Jesus Christ descended.

Betrayal of another person is always activated by selfish motives. Read Luke 22:48 for the most flagrant betrayal of all time. What was Judas' motive according to Luke 22:4–6? ____________

______________________________________________

## Discussion Question

If you've been deeply wounded through the betrayal of another and that person does not seek your forgiveness, is it possible to still forgive him or her? Explain.

## Personal Application Question

Jacob's name was changed from Jacob to Israel, because he was no longer a deceiver. What descriptive name do you think the Lord would give to you and why?

Read Psalm 139:23–24, and spend a few minutes in prayer, asking God to search your heart—to try your thoughts to see if there is any hurtful, offensive, or grievous way in you and to lead you in the way everlasting.

Rachel was an example of the old adage that "love conquers all"—but not always without deep emotional scars along the way. Next week, we will start a new journey through time of over four hundred years and the distance from Bethel to the Land of Goshen in Egypt in order to meet Miriam. Joseph, Jacob's firstborn with Rachel, is our link to our upcoming exciting venture.

[1]Kroon, Rita. *Letters from the Past* (Denver, Colorado: Outskirts Press, 2011), 42.

# Miriam

The Lord heard your grumblings against Him.
—Exodus 16:7 (NIV)

We are introduced to Miriam when she was just seven years old. The Israelite people had been slaves in captivity in Egypt for over three centuries, and because the Israelite people were becoming too numerous, Pharaoh decreed that all Hebrew baby boys were to be killed. Miriam's brother, Moses, was one of these babies. However, to save the infant from death, Miriam's mother and Miriam made a little waterproof basket, put Moses into it, and placed it among the reeds of the royal bathing area of the Nile River. Miriam hid among the reeds to watch.

When Pharaoh's daughter discovered the basket with the crying baby, Miriam bravely stepped forward and asked if she should get a Hebrew woman to nurse the infant. Her wish was granted, so Miriam ran to get her mother. An agreement was made between the two women that the baby would be returned to Pharaoh's daughter after he was weaned.

When that time occurred, the small, young lad was taken into Pharaoh's family (Exodus 2:2–10). We marvel at the ingenuity, courage, and leadership displayed by Miriam in rescuing the youngest of her two brothers. We don't hear of Miriam again until she is eighty-seven years old when the Lord delivered the people of Israel from four hundred years of bondage in Egypt.

After Moses spent forty years in Egypt and forty years in Midian, God called him from ________

______________________________________________________________________

that was not consumed (Exodus 3:2). "I will send you to Pharaoh so that you may bring My people, the sons of Israel, out of Egypt … Thus you shall say, 'I AM has sent you'" (Exodus 3:10, 14). After

making several excuses to the Lord, including the excuse that he was not an eloquent speaker, and after the Lord's anger burned against him, Moses returned to Egypt. With what words of the Lord did the discussion between the Lord and Moses end abruptly? (Exodus 4:14)________________

________________________________________

Pharaoh's heart was hardened, and he would not let the people go. Finally, after God sent numerous plagues, including turning the Nile River and all its streams and pools into blood; swarms of frogs; gnats like the dust of the earth; an infectious and fatal disease of all livestock; painful boils on man and beast; hail and flashes of fire; locusts; darkness so dark it could be felt; and the final and most devastating plague, the death of the firstborn of all the Egyptians, Pharaoh relented and agreed to let the people go. However, because the Israelites dwelt in Goshen in the northeast corner of the land, they were spared the plagues, and since they applied the blood of the sacrificial lamb over their doorposts as commanded, they were also spared the death of their firstborn as the angel of death passed over.

According to John 1:29, who is the Lamb of God, and what was His purpose? ________________

________________________________________

________________________________________

Those who have their sins forgiven under the blood of the Lamb are spared eternal death. The exodus from Egypt is a beautiful picture that correlates to the shed blood of Jesus Christ and provides the way of escape of eternal death.

Picture 603,000 men, aside from women and children, escaping captivity under the mighty hand of God! Since the census at Sinai showed only males twenty years and older, if that represented one fourth of the population, then there were very likely around two million people on the move! God led the mass of people around by the way of the wilderness to the Red Sea to avoid the Philistines. But Pharaoh and his army were in hot pursuit!

When the sons of Israel saw the Egyptian army marching after them, they cried out to the Lord. But Moses exclaimed, "Do not fear! The Lord will fight for you while you keep silent" (Exodus 14:13–14). But the Egyptian army pursued the Israelites to the Red Sea. With the Egyptian army behind them and the Red Sea before them, the people of Israel had nowhere to turn.

But then God did an amazing thing! He told Moses to stretch out his hands over the water, and as he did so, what happened? (Exodus 14:16) ________________________________

Huge walls of water stood up, allowing the sea of people to pass over on dry land. When they reached the other side safely, Moses was to hold his hands over the water once again as the Egyptian chariots and horses and their riders pursued. Suddenly the walls of water crashed over the Egyptians, drowning

the entire army. The Lord saved Israel that day, and Israel *saw* the Egyptians dead on the seashore (Exodus 14:30).

The people of Israel stood in awe of the Lord and sang a song of deliverance. Miriam, the prophetess, led the women in song and dance in response to their song. "Sing to the Lord, for He is highly exalted; the horse and his rider He has hurled into the sea" (Exodus 15:21). We join in celebration as Miriam's leadership capabilities once again came to the forefront. But the celebration was short-lived.

After three days, what problem did the Israelites encounter? (Exodus 15:22)____________________
How did they react? (Exodus 15:24) ________________________________________

Webster's Dictionary defines *grumble* as "to mutter or mumble in discontent; to complain in a surly or peevish manner."

God led the people to twelve springs of water and seventy date palms. And the people were refreshed. But on the fifteenth day of the second month after their departure from Egypt, what did the people grumble about? (Exodus 16:3) ________________________________________
________________________________ What did God provide for them? (Exodus 16:4)
________________________________________________________; also known as
________________________________________________________ (Exodus 16:31)

The people traveled in stages, and when they reached Rephidim, what did the people complain about? (Exodus 17:1) ________________________________________ Moses was exasperated with their constant grumbling and complaining and asked, "Why do you quarrel with me and why do you test the Lord?" (Exodus 17:2) The people quarreled, saying, "Is the Lord among us, or not?" From where did God provide water? (Exodus 17:6) ______________________________

Read Numbers 11:4–6. What did the rabble complain about? __________________ What did God provide? (Numbers 11:31) ____________________ While the meat was still between their teeth, the anger of the Lord was kindled against the greedy mob (Numbers 11:33).

God commanded people not to "test the Lord," "put God to the test," "tempt God," or "try the Lord" with grumbling and complaining. See Deuteronomy 6:16; Psalm 78:18, 41; Matthew 4:7; and 1 Corinthians 10:9.

One commentator writes,

> I think that this is something that we need to take into account when we're prone to complain about our lot in life. Who is it that has brought me here? Any complaining

> that I do is in reality complaining against God. For God is the one who has brought me to these circumstances. God is the one who has placed me here, *unless* I've been disobedient to Him. But my complaints are really against the Lord, and that's a very serious thing, to be complaining against God.[1]

Listen to what the Lord said about grumbling in Numbers 14:27, 29: "How long shall I bear with this evil congregation who are grumbling against Me? I have heard the complaints of the sons of Israel, which they are making against Me ... your corpses shall fall in this wilderness, even all your numbered men, according to your complete number from twenty years old and upward who have grumbled against Me." Obviously, grumbling is a grievous sin against the Lord, since over six hundred thousand men died during the forty years in the wilderness.

While Moses was on Mount Sinai for forty days, receiving the Ten Commandments, the people became restless and impatient. What did they do? (Exodus 32:8) ______________________________
______________________________ What incredulous statement did Aaron make? (Exodus 32:4)
______________________________________________________________
______________________________________________________________

Idolatry is anything or anyone who takes the rightful place of God. Webster's Dictionary defines it as "the worship of idols."

Read Colossians 3:5–8. Colossians 3:5 says, "Put to death, therefore, whatever belongs to your earthly nature; immorality, impurity, lust, evil desires, and greed, which is idolatry." Do you have a golden calf in your life? How has your golden calf usurped the rightful place of God in your heart?

Idolatry, when joined with grumbling, becomes a lethal playmate! Things go from bad to worse when immorality and greed link claws with the deadly duo. Soon jealousy and criticism lash out.

*Criticism* is "the act of finding fault or disapproving of a person or thing" according to Webster's Dictionary.

Let's fall into step with Miriam. We note that Moses' job was no small task and that he needed all the encouragement and support he could get. "I alone am not able to carry all this people because it is too burdensome for me," Moses said (Numbers 11:14). Even though the Lord provided seventy elders to help Moses, imagine what would happen to Moses' confidence—as well as the confidence of the people—if members of Moses' own family undermined his leadership by criticizing him in public! That is exactly what happened. Read Numbers 12:1–2. What did Miriam say? ____________
______________________________________________________________
______________________________________________________________

The verb *spoke* is feminine singular, indicating that Miriam led in this criticism out of jealousy and envy for the high position to which the Lord had called Moses.

And the Lord heard it! (Numbers 12:2)

At once, the Lord commanded Moses, Aaron, and Miriam, "Come out to the Tent of Meeting, all three of you" (Numbers 12:4). The Lord affirmed Moses as His humble servant ("Moses, My servant, is faithful in all My household") and then asked Miriam and Aaron, "Why then were you not afraid to speak against My servant, against Moses?" And the anger of the Lord burned against Miriam and Aaron, and He departed. What happened immediately after His departure? (Numbers 12:10)_____

________________________________________________

Since leprosy was a very serious and contagious disease, Miriam was shut outside the camp for seven days according to the laws governing leprosy. Can you envision the shame and guilt she must have felt?

So far, we've witnessed the people grumbling and complaining numerous times against God for His provision for them; worshipping and sacrificing to a golden calf with out-of-control immorality and much drinking; greed and quarrelling; and Miriam's jealousy and envy, leading to public criticism of God's chosen servant! Do you see how all of this rebellion is directed toward God and why it stirs up His wrath?

With all the sin of the people of Israel in the wilderness comes a refreshing breath of air. Moses and Aaron pleaded with the Lord on behalf of Miriam, and after her week of isolation, she was restored. What a beautiful picture of our own restoration to God through the reconciling work of Jesus Christ on the cross! "For if while we were enemies we were reconciled to God by the death of his Son, much more, now that we are reconciled, shall we be saved by his life" (Romans 5:10).

Many of us may not recognize our bent to grumble and to complain, commit idolatry, be jealous, or criticize, but unless we are perfect, the bent is there!

## Discussion Question

What insight did you gain from the examples of grumbling and complaining that you can apply to your own responses to unpleasant situations? "Since it is God who is at work in you, both to will and to work for His good pleasure," (Philippians 2:13) ought we not do all things without grumbling and complaining? (Philippians 4:13–14) Shouldn't we give thanks in everything, knowing that this is God's will for us in Christ Jesus? (1 Thessalonians 5:18) Shouldn't we cultivate a joyful heart as good medicine for our soul? (Proverbs 17:22) The next time we are with friends, before the conversation

turns to everyday grumbling and complaining, imagine what would happen if we asked, "What is God doing in your life?"

"Those who belong to Christ have crucified the flesh along with its passions and desires" (Galatians 5:24) Shouldn't we seek to be grateful, give praise, and find peace even in troubled times?

We may admire Miriam for her bravery, ingenuity, and leadership, but we can also identify with her in times of grumbling, complaining, and being critical, wouldn't you agree? In the times we find fault with someone and criticize him or her, should we rather remind ourselves that in the same way we judge another, we will be judged (Matthew 7:2), and if we bite and devour one another, we will be devoured? (Galatians 5:15) Wouldn't it be better if we put on a heart of compassion, kindness, humility, gentleness, and patience, bearing with one another and forgiving each other? (Colossians 3:12–13) Ought we not to love our neighbor as ourselves? (Matthew 22:39) Shouldn't we seek the Lord in prayer as we strive to overcome whatever obstacles loom before us?

## Discussion Question

Contrast valid insight with a loving spirit (truth in love) and being openly critical.

## Personal Application Question

Recall times you may have been critical of another person. What do you think may have been an underlying attitude in your heart that sparked the criticism?

Since we are all called by God to love Him with all hearts, minds, and strength and to love others as ourselves (Luke 10:27), how should our response change the next time we are tempted to grumble and complain?

*Prayer:* Show me Your way, Lord, that I may know You and know what pleases You (Exodus 33:13). When I grumble and complain, open my eyes to Your goodness, grace and mercy so that I may give praise and thanksgiving. Give me a heart of love and compassion so that I may not be critical of another. Lead me in the way I ought to go for Your name's sake.

[1]Smith, Chuck, *Exodus 16-18* (Costa Mesa, CA: The Word For Today, 2000)

# DEBORAH

Trust in the LORD with all your heart, and do not lean on your own understanding.
—Proverbs 3:5

Though the Promised Land had been generally conquered and occupied by the people of Israel after their miraculous delivery from Egypt and their forty years in the wilderness, certain Canaanite strongholds still remained. Consequently, the enemy became an entrapment for the sons of Israel and a constant source of idol worship influence. Therefore, the Lord's anger was kindled against the Israelites, and He often gave them into the hands of their enemies. The Israelites would be oppressed for years at a time. God's faithfulness was not based on the obedience of His people; rather, the enjoyment of His blessings was conditioned on their obedience to Him.

The command to love the Lord found in Deuteronomy 6:5 says, "You shall love the Lord your God with all your heart and with all your soul and with all your might." When Jesus was asked by one of the Pharisees, "Which is the great commandment in the Law," how did Jesus respond according to Matthew 22:37?________________________________________

____________________________________________________

Israel had been commanded to utterly destroy the Canaanites when they took possession of the Promised Land. "You shall defeat them, then you shall utterly destroy them. You shall make no covenant with them and to show no favor to them. Furthermore, you shall not intermarry with them; you shall not give your daughters to their sons, nor shall you take their daughters for your sons." Why? See Deuteronomy 7:4.________________________________________

____________________________________________________

____________________________________________________

It was during this turbulent time when every man did what was right in his own eyes (Judges 17:6, 21:25) that the Lord raised up judges to rule over His people (Judges 2:16). Judges served as spiritual, military, and governmental leaders but were often ignored or rejected (Judges 2:17). Each time one of the judges died, the people reverted back to their evil ways, and the Lord delivered them into the hands of their enemies. The era of judges covers the period in Israel's history from about 1380 to 1050 BC. Historically, the book of Judges links the conquest of the Promised Land (Palestine) to the beginnings of the monarchy (kings).

After an evil outbreak of the people of Israel, the Lord sold them into the hand of Jabin, king of Canaan. His commander, Sisera, was skilled and had disciplined soldiers that were armed to the hilt with weapons and iron-trimmed chariots. At just the mention of Sisera's name, terror spread like black storm clouds over the land. It was reported that the mighty Canaanite army possessed nine hundred chariots ready for battle.[1] For twenty years, Israel was severely oppressed. It was at this time and place in history that we meet Deborah, the fourth judge to rule over Israel.

Read Judges 4:4. Deborah was known as a __________ and was ____________ to a man named Lappidoth. Her judge's chambers, where she presided over civil matters, consisted of palm trees and open space. One tree in particular became known as the Palm of Deborah (Deuteronomy 4:5). As a prophetess, Deborah did not foretell future events; rather, she would hear a message from God and simply and obediently repeat the words of God to the people. These were usually words of warning to separate themselves from the wicked people around them, especially in the hill country of Ephraim; sometimes they were words of military strategy. Deborah recognized that she had no authority of her own but only that which had been given her by God.[2] Deborah also commanded the military. Who was her right-hand military man? (Judges 4:6) ________________________________________

One day, the Lord spoke to Deborah concerning a military matter. According to Judges 4:6–7, Deborah then summoned Barak and said, "Behold, the Lord, the God of Israel, has commanded, 'Go and march to Mount Tabor, and take with you ten thousand men from the sons of Naphtali and from the sons of Zebulun. And I will draw out to you Sisera with his chariots and his many troops to the river Kishon and I will give him into your hand.'" Notice how Deborah prefaced her orders to Barak: "the Lord, the God of Israel, has commanded."

Even though Barak heard the words of the Lord, "I will give him into your hands," he saw that the enemy had nine hundred iron chariots and all the people to go with them in addition to the foot soldiers! (Judges 4:3) From Barak's perspective, Israel had only ill-equipped foot soldiers against a vast army with nine hundred iron chariots! What did he say to Deborah? (Judges 4:8)__________ ____________________________________________ Read Judges 4:9. (Although the tribes of Reuben, Gilead, Dan, and Asher refused to join in the battle against their enemy, the warriors of Ephraim, Benjamin, and Issachar, did follow in the battle [Judges 5:14–17].)

But the Lord caused a deluge the night before the battle, causing the Kishon River to overflow its banks, rendering the chariots useless in the mud and muck. When Deborah saw what the Lord had done, she said to Barak, "Arise! For this is the day in which the Lord has given Sisera into your hands!" With those words of encouragement ringing in his ears, the battle began. Israel defeated the enemy; Sisera was the only one to escape—but not for long.

Sisera fled on foot to the tent of Heber and his wife, Jael, begging for protection. But after giving Sisera some milk to drink and covering him with a blanket, Jael drove a tent stake through his temple, killing him as he slept. Read Judges 4:9.

According to Judges 4:23, who subdued Jabin, king of Canaan? ____________ Then Deborah and Barak sang poetic songs of praise to the Lord for His deliverance of the people of Israel against their enemy. The land had peace for forty years under Deborah's rule as judge over Israel prior her death.

Several other judges ruled over Israel, including Gideon and Samson. After every judge died, the people of Israel would do evil in the sight of the Lord, and the Lord would again deliver them into the hands of their enemies. After one such time of affliction, the people of Israel cried out to be delivered. What was the Lord's response to one such outcry as found in Judges 10:13–14? ________________

________________________________________________________________________

________________________________________________________________________

________________________________________________________________________

________________________________________________________________________

The people of Israel confessed their sin, put away their foreign gods, and cried out to be delivered once again. After the Lord recapped the many times He had delivered the sons of Israel from Egypt and from the hands of their many enemies, the Lord "could bear the misery of Israel no longer" (Judges 10:16). So once again, He delivered the people of Israel under Judge Japhthah.

Judges 17:6, 21:25 appropriately summarizes the era of judges: there was no king to rule over Israel, and everyone did what was right in his own eyes. If left to ourselves with no governing body, whether it is government law or family discipline, man always seems to run amuck, don't you agree? The end result is always chaos and flagrant evil, as we will see when we meet Tamar in our next week's lesson.

As Deborah has set a beautiful example for us as an obedient, trusting woman of faith in her calling as judge over Israel, she brought glory and honor to the God she served. I hope you enjoyed our time with Deborah as much as I did. Remember, our greatest calling is to glorify Jesus Christ, and we bring glory to the Father when we trust Him in all things.

What does God require of us in order for us to be called of God? Write Psalm 46:10. __________

________________________________________

________________________________________

What must we do to be an effective servant of the Lord God Almighty? Write Proverbs 3:5 ______

________________________________________

________________________________________

## Discussion Question

Discuss the characteristics you would ascribe to Deborah and why.

| | |
|---|---|
| ______ Brave | ______ Trusts in the Lord |
| ______ Intelligent | ______ Prideful |
| ______ Fickle | ______ Shy |
| ______ Obedient to the Lord | ______ Assured |
| ______ Fearless | ______ Poetic and musical |

## Personal Application Question:

What battle/obstacle are you facing? Prepare for yourself a battle plan. [1]Identify the enemy. [2]Pray for guidance and protection. [3]Trust in God's promises. [4]Read and believe the corresponding verses. [5]Act in faith. If your enemy is one of the areas described below, read the corresponding verse.

| | |
|---|---|
| Satan—Colossians 2:15 | Guilt—1 Corinthians 1:7–9 |
| Pride—Ephesians 2:9–10 | Hopelessness—Romans 8:38–39 |
| Doubt—1 John 3:1 | Greed—Philippians 3:8 |
| Hate—Ephesians 4:32 | Fear—Romans 8:15 |
| Apathy—Titus 2:14 | Unbelief—Mark 9:24 |

Take a few minutes to write a prayer, asking God for an added measure of faith in order to trust and obey Him as He calls you to make a difference in the life of another, your family, your church, or your community.

## Notes

[1]Kroon, Rita. *Letters from the Past* (Denver, Colorado: Outskirts Press, 2011), 108.

[2]Kroon, Rita. *Letters from the Past* (Denver, Colorado: Outskirts Press, 2011), 107.

# TAMAR

A bruised reed He will not break, and a dimly burning candle He will not extinguish.
—Isaiah 42:3

Before we greet Tamar, let's meet her father. David, the youngest of his seven brothers, was a handsome lad with beautiful eyes, but he mostly went unnoticed as he shepherded his father's sheep in Bethlehem. But God noticed David, and He chose David to reign as king over Israel.

David did not seek to be king; he didn't have to. He was called by God and anointed by Samuel, the prophet. The Lord said to Samuel, "Arise, anoint him; for this is he" (1 Samuel 16:12).

David did not become king at that time, however. He had to wait until he was thirty years old. In the meantime, he served Saul, the first king over Israel. Since David was a skilled musician, he played the harp and sang for Saul when Saul was troubled during times of depression. David succeeded in all he did, for the Lord God of hosts was with him (2 Samuel 5:10). It was through many battles, victories, threats on his life, and escapes that David also became a mighty warrior—a man of valor.

Saul turned away from the Lord. One day, during a particularly fierce battle, at age seventy-two, he was wounded and fell on his own sword and died. David became king in Saul's place and first ruled from Jerusalem over Judah for seven and a half years and then over Israel for another thirty three years. It was during this reign of King David that we meet his daughter, Tamar.

David married several wives and had many concubines. This was in direct violation of Deuteronomy 17:15–20, which clearly spelled out the conditions of a king over Israel—[1]to be chosen by God, [2]to be an Israelite, [3]not to imitate royal courts of other nations in his desire for horses, wives, and money,

and [4]to have a copy of the Law and obey it. But in ancient times, international alliances were often sealed by the marriage of a king's daughter to the other participant in the treaty, so David had many sons and daughters. His oldest son was Amnon. (Tuck this name in the forefront of your memory, as Amnon plays an important role in our study.)

One such political marriage was between David and Maacha, daughter of Talmai, king of the neighboring kingdom of Geshur. David had two children with Maacha—Absalom, his third-oldest son, and Tamar. What two words describe Tamar according to 2 Samuel 13:1–2? ____________ and ____________________________________________

Tamar's heritage was one of royalty. Her father was King David, and her mother was the daughter of a king. This made Tamar a true princess, but that did not protect her from an unspeakable tragedy that changed her life forever.

Beloved, I want to be extremely sensitive and very tenderhearted to those of you who may have been deeply wounded or victimized by a perpetrator—sexually, verbally, emotionally, or physically. I certainly do not want to cause undue heartache or stir up painful memories. On the contrary, I hope today's lesson will lend encouragement and bring healing as we pursue a very tragic and life-changing event in Tamar's life.

Amnon thought he loved Tamar, but in actuality, he lusted for her, even though incest was as strictly forbidden in their culture, as it is in our culture today. Second Samuel 13:2 says, "And Amnon was so frustrated (sexually) because of his sister Tamar that he made himself __________, for she was a virgin and it seemed hard to Amnon to do anything to her."

Amnon had a shrewd and unscrupulous cousin named Jonadab who came up with a plan to get Tamar to come to Amnon's bedroom, where he could have his way with her. Amnon was to feign illness, and then he was to request that Tamar come to him, prepare cakes for him, and feed them to him. What further action did Amnon take? See 2 Samuel 13:9. ________________________

________________________________________________________

Then he commanded Tamar to bring the food to him in his bedroom. It was at this point that Amnon grabbed Tamar and forced himself upon her, violating her as she struggled and pleaded in vain.

What immediate effect did this act have on Amnon? (2 Samuel 13:15) ____________________

________________________________________________________

How commonplace for lust, once gratified, to turn to hate! Rapists have nothing more than hostility and disdain for those they have victimized. They care nothing at all for the irreparable harm they have caused to another human being. And that is exactly what Amnon felt for Tamar! Listen to Amnon's

words to his young male attendant in 2 Samuel 13:17: "Now throw this woman out of my presence, and lock the door behind her."

Throw this woman out? Compare his reference to Tamar with 2 Samuel 13:6, where he said, "Please let my sister, Tamar, come and make me a couple of cakes." Do you hear his disdain for Tamar?

What did Tamar do? (2 Samuel 13:19) ____________________

____________________

____________________

Tamar was clearly traumatized, wailing and tearing her clothes as she ran. There were no police to call, no one to comfort her, and no one to come to her aid. She was alone in her despair. She was desperate in her need.

Amidst her tears, loud cries, and torn clothing, Tamar ran into her brother, Absalom. What shocking words did he say to her? (2 Samuel 13:20) ____________________

____________________

____________________

Keep silent? Pretend this never happened? Don't do anything rash? What about Leviticus 20:17, which says, "If there is a man who takes his sister, his father's daughter or his mother's daughter, so that he sees her nakedness and she sees his nakedness, it is a disgrace; and they shall be cut off in the sight of the sons of their people"? What about Deuteronomy 27:22, which says, "Cursed is he who lies with his sister, the daughter of his father or of his mother"? Surely Absalom knew of this command, don't you agree? However, Absalom took Tamar into his home, where she remained in seclusion, but nothing was done to Amnon—nothing except for the secret revenge Absalom plotted against Amnon, that is.

What about Tamar's father? How did he react when he heard the news? (2 Samuel 13:21) ________ ____________________ But he did nothing to vindicate his daughter! Could it be that David did nothing to Amnon, his firstborn son, for the rape of Tamar, because the punishment would have meant death for Amnon? Or could it be that it meant death for *both* Amnon and Tamar? What if David remembered his own adulterous affair with Bathsheba? Even though he repented, was forgiven, and was spared death from his sexual immorality, did he think he could rightfully inflict punishment on Amnon? (2 Samuel 12:13) Whatever the reason, Tamar was left devastated—a desolate woman. Webster's Dictionary defines *desolate* as "left alone; lonely; solitary." There is no evidence that indicates that Tamar was ever anything but a desolate woman for the rest of her life. Tamar was judged and ostracized by family and friends for something that was not her fault.

How fitting are the words her father had written of himself in Psalm 69.

> I have sunk in deep mire! There is no foothold. I have come into deep waters, and a flood overflows me. I am weary with my crying; my throat is parched. Those who hate me without a cause are more than the hairs of my head. Those who would destroy me are powerful. Dishonor has covered my face. I have become estranged from my brothers and as an alien to my brothers. I wept in my soul and it became my reproach. I made sackcloth of my clothing and I became a byword to those who sit in the gate who talk about me. I am the song of the drunkards. Reproach has broken my heart. I look for sympathy, but there was none; and for comforters, I have found none.

However, Psalm 34:15–22 leads me to believe that Tamar was comforted by the Lord Himself. Would you agree? Write the words of Psalm 34:15–22, and let the meaning of those verses sink deeply into your soul. ____________________________________________

When a person is victimized, he or she oftentimes is labeled. For instance, Tamar may have been labeled "the rape victim." Labeling one who has been victimized only adds a negative identification to that person and continues to hold such a one in bondage. Hurtful labels can isolate and imprison one as much as physical seclusion does. It is better to say that Tamar was raped, but she was still a young woman who was worthy of compassion, tender care, and loving arms. Seek the Lord as you help begin the process of healing one who was devastated by rape or any other extreme abuse of the body, mind, or soul. Seek professional counseling. Reassure the one victimized that the abuse was not his or her fault. Come alongside the one who was victimized. Validate this person and his or her feelings as you lead him or her to the one who "will wipe away every tear from their eyes, and death shall be no more, neither shall there be mourning, nor crying, nor pain anymore, for the former things have passed away" (Revelation 21:4, ESV). Remember to pray, pray, pray.

Being victimized by rape leaves one feeling dirty and worthless. A repentant sinner may feel the same uncleanness, but our heavenly Father cleanses us and turns our darkness into light. "Purify me with hyssop, and I shall be clean; wash me, and I shall be whiter than snow. Make me to hear joy and gladness" (Psalm 51:7–8). There is hope for healing! There is freedom in forgiving!

Forgiveness does not necessarily mean a restored relationship (if there was one previously), but it does mean freeing oneself from becoming victimized again. Becoming victimized by bitterness, hatred, and anger toward the perpetrator may incapacitate a person almost as much as the perpetrated crime does.

Beloved, do not let your past dictate who you are; let it be part of who you will become!

I know this was a difficult and sensitive stop on our journey, but nevertheless, it is one that is vital to our study of women of the Old Testament. It is my prayer that as we spent time with Tamar, you were able to find resolve and healing if you or a loved one was victimized in any way.

## Discussion Question

Do you know of a friend who was traumatized in one way or another and does not want to talk about it, since the wound is too deep or the shame is too great? If you sense that she is being crushed by the burden, what would be a sensitive and appropriate way for you to help her to begin the healing process?

## Personal Application Question

Think about this—if you were the one victimized, would you want the perpetrator to be punished according to man's law or God's standard of justice? Why? ____________________

____________________

____________________

____________________

Would you be more prone to seek revenge or justice? ____________________

Why? ____________________

____________________

____________________

Beloved, do you not know that the evil one will stand before a righteous judge and give an account of his every deed? His punishment will certainly fit the evil done to the innocent. What does Romans 14:12 say? ______________________________

______________________________

______________________________

Take a few minutes, and write your own psalm, expressing to the Lord what is on your heart. Include praise to the Lord for His care, concern, and love for you.

Our last stop of our journey takes us to Persia, where we will meet and dine with Esther.

## *Notes*

# Esther

"Who knows whether you have not attained royalty for such a time as this?"
—Esther 4:14

The heritage of God's chosen nation, Israel, is one of blessing and woe, peace and war—but the people of Israel were always a people of promise. The Jews had been in captivity for seventy years in Babylon under King Nebuchadnezzar when Babylon was overthrown by Cyrus, King of Persia. The area under his control was from India to Ethiopia (present-day Pakistan and North Sudan). King Cyrus issued a decree allowing the displaced peoples to return to their homelands, and many did return, but for reasons unknown to us, many of the Jews remained in exile in Persia. Esther was such an exile.

Esther was a young orphan girl who had been adopted by her older cousin, Mordecai, an honorable, caring, and gentle man. (Esther was her Persian name, but in Hebrew, her name was Hadassah.)

When Esther was about ten years old, a new king began his reign in Persia. His Greek name was Xerxes; in Hebrew, it was Ahasuerus. After a time, he lavishly displayed "the riches of his royal glory and the splendor of his great majesty" for an amazing six months! (Esther 1:4) All the princes of his 127 provinces, the army officers, and the nobles attended this gala event.

At the conclusion, a seven-day drinking feast was held by the king for all the people who were present in Susa, the capital (Esther 1:5). It was on the last day of this banquet that the drunken king ordered Queen Vashti to appear in her royal robes in order to parade her before the people so that they may see her beauty. What did Queen Vashti do? See Esther 1:12. ________________
In King Ahasuerus' anger and on the counsel of his wise men, the king divorced his beautiful

queen. In addition, the king issued a decree that every man should be the master in his own house (Esther 1:22).

Can you imagine what it may have been like for a young Jewish girl growing up in a land where there was a king and a queen? Perhaps Esther had a fairytale dream of becoming a beautiful queen herself, wearing royal robes and exquisite jewels fit only for a queen. Could the divorce of her beautiful queen have crushed her dreams of the splendor of being a queen? Do you remember childhood dreams of make-believe? What were your dreams, and how have your dreams changed as you matured? _____

______________________________________________________________

______________________________________________________________

______________________________________________________________

After a time, the king longed for ex-queen Vashti. To console the king, what did his attendants suggest? (Esther 2:2) ______________________________________________

______________________________________________________________

______________________________________________________________

______________________________________________________________

As a teenage girl, Esther was also brought to the palace and placed in the harem. Mordecai had instructed Esther not to reveal her kindred people or her Hebrew name, and Esther was careful to obey.

Every day, Mordecai would walk back and forth in front of the court of the harem to learn how Esther fared (Esther 2:11). Do you think Esther felt safe with her father-figure cousin watching over her? We can have the same security knowing that our heavenly Father watches over us.

When it was Esther's turn to go before the king, how did the king respond to her? (Esther 2:17) ___

______________________________________________________________

______________________________________________________________

One day, as Mordecai sat in his customary place in the palace gate, he overheard two gate keepers plot to kill the king. Mordecai immediately sent word to Esther, urging her to tell the king. The plot was investigated and found to be true, and the two would-be assassins were hung. The incident was recorded in the presence of the king in the book of the Chronicles of the Kings of Media and Persia (Esther 2:23), but nothing more was done.

Four years after Esther was made queen, King Ahasuerus promoted a spiteful and egotistical man named Haman to be in authority over all the princes. At the king's command, all the servants at the king's gate were to bow down and pay homage to Haman.

Haman became puffed up with pride, so when Mordecai did not bow down to him, Haman became furious! What simple reason did Mordecai give the servants when asked why he did not bow to Haman? (Esther 3:4) "I am a ______________________________."

Haman realized that to kill only Mordecai would not solve his problem; he had to destroy *all* the Jews. An evil plan began to formulate in his mind; he was driven to near madness by thoughts of how to accomplish his plan. He wasted no time in going to the king. What did Haman say to the king? (Esther 3:8–9)______________________________

______________________________

______________________________

______________________________

______________________________

The king did not bother to ask who these people were that had different laws and refused to obey the king's orders. King Ahasuerus simply gave Haman his signet ring "to do with them as you please" (Esther 3:11). What is Haman called in Esther 3:10? ______________________________

______________________________

Haman devised an evil plot to annihilate all the Jews! The edict went out to all the provinces, and there was a great commotion just outside the palace. Esther heard of the uproar and wailing and sent her attendant to learn the cause.

Mordecai told the attendant of the plan to destroy the Jews and then sent a copy of the edict back to Esther, imploring her to go to the king. Esther was distressed, to say the least, but her immediate concern was going before the king without being summoned. "Any man or woman who comes to the king in the inner court who was not summoned, there is but one law; that he be put to death, unless the king holds out to him the golden scepter" (Esther 4:11). The relay race was on, with messages darting back and forth between Esther and Mordecai as they discussed to how to handle this crisis.

Esther risked death whether she approached the king or not. Listen to Mordecai's profound words recorded in Esther 4:13–14. "For if you remain silent at this time, relief and deliverance will arise for the Jews from another place and you and your father's house will perish. And who knows whether you have not attained royalty for such a time as this?"

The realization that perhaps this was the reason she, an orphan Jewish girl, became queen over Persia penetrated her soul like a knife! That in itself was a preposterous chain of events! Esther told Mordecai to assemble the Jews and fast for three days, and she and her maidens would do likewise. At the end of three days, she would put on her royal robes and stand in the throne room opposite the entrance to the palace inner court, "and if I perish, I perish" (Esther 4:16).

What secret did the apostle Paul discover for obtaining inner peace and strength in every circumstance? (Philippians 4:13) ____________________________________________

____________________________________________

____________________________________________

____________________________________________

After three days of fasting, Esther put on her royal robes and stood in the inner court of the king's rooms. The king extended the golden scepter to her, and she touched its top. He asked her what her request was. Esther replied that she would like to have Haman and the king attend a banquet that she would prepare for them the following day.

At the banquet, the king asked Esther again what her request was. She extended the same invitation to yet another banquet she would prepare the next day. Of course, both the king and Haman accepted her invitation.

Haman was pleased of heart as left the banquet—until he saw Mordecai and Mordecai did not bow to him, that is. Haman became infuriated and grumbled about this matter to his wife and his friends. Haman's wife suggested that Haman have a gallows built, and in the morning, ask the king to have Mordecai hanged on it, "then go joyfully with the king to the banquet." (Esther 5:14)

That night, the king could not sleep, so he ordered that the book of the chronicles be read to him. When the king heard the account of Mordecai foiling the attempted assassination on his life by the two gate keepers, he asked what had been done to honor Mordecai. "Nothing," came the servants' reply. When the king asked who was in the court, he was told that Haman was. "Bring him in," the king said.

The king asked Haman what special tribute should be bestowed on someone the king wished to honor. Naturally, Haman thought the king was referring to him, so he said that such a one should be led around the city square, riding on the king's own horse, wearing a royal robe that the king had worn, and wearing a crown. It was to be proclaimed, "Thus it shall be done to the man whom the king desires to honor" (Esther 6:8–9). The king agreed and said to do exactly what he said to Mordecai! After Haman's reluctant display of honor towards Mordecai, Mordecai returned to the king's gate, and Haman went home sulking.

As Haman recounted to his wife and his friends everything that had happened, his wife and friends apparently suspected that if Mordecai was a Jew, it would mean certain doom for Haman; hence, her words in Esther 6:13: "If Mordecai, before whom you have begun to fall, is of Jewish origin, you will not overcome him, but will surely fall before him.." While Haman's wife was still speaking these words of dire straits to Haman, the king's eunuchs arrived to escort Haman to the banquet.

The situation went from bad to worse for Haman when at the banquet, the king again asked Esther what her request was. Queen Esther revealed Haman's evil plot to destroy the Jews. The king became furious and stormed out to the palace garden. Meanwhile, Haman fell onto the couch, begging Esther for his life. The king reentered the room and exclaimed, "Will he even assault the queen with me in the house?" As soon as he spoke these words, his servants covered Haman's face. One of the servants told the king of the gallows Haman had built on which to hang Mordecai. "Hang Haman on it!" the king ordered. So they hanged Haman, and the king's anger subsided.

Webster's Dictionary defines *poetic justice* as "justice in which good is properly rewarded and evil punished; justice as one might wish it to be." *Irony* is defined as "a combination of circumstances or a result that is the opposite of what is or might be expected or considered appropriate."

On the same day poetic justice was served, Esther inherited Haman's house. She also disclosed to King Ahasuerus how Mordecai was related to her, admitting her Jewish heritage. She then asked if the original decree could be nullified. It could not. But a new decree could be issued, giving the Jews the right to defend themselves against their enemies. So Esther and Mordecai drafted up the new decree, and there was a great celebration among the Jews.

There are many similarities and differences between the decree Haman issued and the decree God issued. Let's unpack several of these similarities and differences. The main similarity between the decree issued by Haman and the decree issued by God is that both edicts decreed death.

Haman's decree for death was simply because the people were Jews. God's decree for death was exclusively because of sin. "The soul who sins will die" (Ezekiel 18:4, NASB). Write Romans 6:23. _

___

___

___

A simple comparison of differences between these two decrees shows that Haman's decree was one that demonstrated partiality; God's decree was one that manifested impartiality. Haman's decree involved only Jews; God's decree was for all mankind. Write Romans 3:23. ___

___

___

Haman issued his decree because he hated the Jews—one Jew in particular, Mordecai. God declared His decree because he hated sin and what it did to the people whom He loved. "There are six things which the Lord hates, yes, seven which are an abomination to Him: haughty eyes, a lying tongue, hands that shed innocent blood, a heart that devises wicked plans, feet that run rapidly to evil, a false witness who utters lies, and one who spreads strife among brothers" (Proverbs 6:16–19).

Neither Haman's decree nor God's decree could be revoked. Haman would not and could not revoke his decree because of his hatred; God could not and would not revoke His decree because of His holiness. "And so I will show my greatness and my holiness, and I will make myself known in the sight of many nations. Then they will know that I am the LORD" (Ezekiel 38:23, NIV).

Both decrees brought death to their authors. Haman was hung on a gallows; Jesus, God's Son, was hung on a cross. Haman's death was to no avail. Jesus Christ's death gave life. Write John 5:21. ___

_______________________________________________

_______________________________________________

_______________________________________________

Haman's law was amended, thereby providing a way of escape for its intended victims. God's law was fulfilled in Christ Jesus, giving life to its called recipients. "Do not think that I (Jesus) came to abolish the Law or the Prophets; I did not come to abolish, but to fulfill" (Matthew 5:17, NASB). The amended law of Haman's deadly decree gave Jews hope and a reason to celebrate. God's fulfilled law gives all mankind who believe the promise of eternal life and also a reason to dance and to shout for joy. "Then maidens will dance and be glad, young men and old as well. I will turn their mourning into gladness; I will give them comfort and joy instead of sorrow" (Jeremiah 31:13, NIV).

Esther was instrumental in establishing a feast, called the Feast of Purim, commemorating the Jews' deliverance from Haman. This was a two-day celebration and was to be observed by every Jew for all generations. A second letter, written by Esther and Mordecai, established the appointed time with instructions for the times of fasting and the times of lamentations during Purim (Esther 9:31–32).

Mordecai was promoted second *only* to the king and great among the Jews, because he sought the good of his people and was one who spoke for the welfare of his whole nation. This is the second time a Jew was promoted to the second highest office in the land that was not his own; the first was Joseph, the eleventh son of Jacob/Israel, when he was second only to Pharaoh of Egypt.

As judge over Israel, Deborah certainly knew the faithfulness of God and obeyed His words. In faith, she looked to God for deliverance for her people. She was filled with courage and acted upon His leading and direction. She drew from knowledge of repeated past sins of her people and God's continual faithfulness to forgive them and rescue them time and time again.

Today, mankind still rebels against God continually. Yet should we not learn from ancient history and long-ago peoples that God is the same yesterday, today, and forever and is faithful to forgive us our sins for His name's sake, not by works of righteousness that we have done? "But when the kindness of God our Savior and His love for mankind appeared, He saved us, not on the basis of deeds which we have done in righteousness, but according to His mercy" (Titus 3:4–5, NASB).

Esther, like Deborah, was placed in a position to rescue her people. Esther also had to have faith and courage to undertake a seemingly impossible task. Her training in obedience through her older cousin, Mordecai, prepared her to be obedient in a most courageous way when called upon to intercede for her people, who were in a very precarious and deadly situation.

You and I, unlike Esther and Deborah, will probably never be called upon to rescue a nation. What amazes me most is that God would call a woman to do such a heroic task. But then God did not rely on the strength of these women; these women had to rely on His strength, might, and wisdom. However, you and I are called to tasks that are specific to us and to our situations—not specific tasks but tasks specific to us. Do you see the difference?

## Discussion Question

Discuss your thoughts on *poetic justice* and *irony* in the book of Esther. Tell of a situation in your life where you have witnessed poetic justice or irony. How did it affect you?

## Personal Application Question

In the story of Esther, a guilty man built a gallows to hang an innocent man, but guilt was paid for by the guilty one. In the account of Jesus, a guilty man built a cross to hang an innocent man, and guilt was paid for by the innocent one. How does this apply to you?

Take a few minutes to write a prayer based on Romans 12:2, asking that the Lord would transform you through the renewal of your mind so that you may understand the good, acceptable, and perfect will of the Lord.

We bid farewell to Queen Esther and continue to admire her for her courage and determination to do what is right. Her story gives us hope and encouragement that no matter how deep or where our roots have grown, our flowers can bloom in God's sunlight.

Dear Friend,
When we are obedient to the Lord God as He calls us: to "fear the Lord your God, to walk in all His ways and love Him and to serve the Lord your God with all your heart and with all your soul," (Deuteronomy 10:12) then, my beloved, we have become women of virtue. Let your light shine!

What a joy this journey has been! Thank you for all your hard work in preparing for each lesson and for your participation in the discussion questions and personal application questions. I give all the glory to our great God for this opportunity to study His Word together. I trust you have grown in your faith in the one true God and Savior, Jesus Christ, as we journeyed together these past eight weeks.

"The Lord bless you and keep you; the Lord make His face to shine upon you, and be gracious to you; the Lord lift up His countenance on you, and give you peace." (Numbers 6:24-26)

*Rita Kroon*

**WHO CAN FIND A VIRTUOUS WOMAN? FOR HER PRICE IS FAR ABOVE RUBIES.**

# About the Author

Rita Kroon has written

Letters from the Past (biblical historical fiction), You Have Cancer: A Journey through the Valley of the Shadow of Death (the story of her personal journey of faith on the battlefield with cancer), Praying the Scriptures (collection of prayers based on Scripture), children's stories, devotionals, wildlife magazine articles, her own weekly column for area newspaper, poetry, and book reviews.

Rita was first drawn to writing while in high school and believes that in order to be considered a successful Christian author, her writing must first honor the Lord Jesus Christ, and secondly, draw others into a deeper walk of faith with Him through the study of the Scriptures.

She received her associate degree in speech and communications, has attended writers' conferences and participated in creative writing classes, and was an active member in writers' critique groups. Rita is a former member of the Minnesota Christian Writers' Guild

Rita and her husband, Burt, reside in Shoreview, Minnesota and attend Bethlehem Baptist Church in Mounds View, where John Piper pastors. Over the past several years, Rita has been involved in women's ministries, attending and leading women's Bible studies. Rita also works with ESL (English as a Second Language) individuals at their church. Burt is active in the evangelism ministry at Bethlehem Baptist. They have three married daughters and seventeen grandchildren. They are actively involved in each grandchild's life and count each one a blessing.